THE GIRLS THAT GLOWED

MARANDA SILVERTON AND BETH LOWE

ISBN 978-1-68526-798-8 (Paperback)
ISBN 978-1-68526-799-5 (Digital)

Covenant Books
11661 Hwy 707
Murrells Inlet, SC 29576
www.covenantbooks.com

Welcome to our story! This book is a collection of our experiences in Jesus. We believed in Jesus, received his spirit, and then our lives changed and truly began. My name is Beth and the other authors are my sister, Maranda; our mother, Frances; and a friend of ours, Peter. We've included a few other writings by other family members as well. We began having visions and experiences almost immediately after receiving the infilling of the Holy Ghost. The time span has been that of fifty years. Sadly, our mother passed away in 2008; however, she had written down quite a few of her experiences. We wanted to share our lives in Christ because there is so much fear and confusion in the world about receiving and living for our God. That would be the God of Abraham, Isaac, and Jacob and a multitude of Christians around the world.

Every person is capable of having a close relationship with the father through his son Jesus. Receiving the infilling of the Holy Ghost, sometimes called "the baptism of/in the Holy Ghost" or "receiving the gift of the Holy Ghost" is the final step to being born again.

This book will show by example how to truly receive the Holy Ghost/Spirit, live holy, and walk the holy life here in a world belonging to Lucifer, the Satan.

The life of the apostles and the saints of the book of Acts did not end. It is still being lived by people like us. There are millions of people around the world that have received the infilling of the Holy Ghost. Not all live a holy life, but a holy life is possible. The word *holy* means "separated from sin." We can all be separated from sin to have experiences with the father of lights (James 1:17 KJV).

BETH

When I would verbally tell someone of spiritual experiences, they would say, "I wish you'd write them all down. I'd love to read them!" I had begun to think that maybe more than a few friends would benefit from not only my experiences, but my sister and my mother's as well, for we each had incredible things happen concerning the Lord Jesus. We each wrote down our most favorite experiences, and they may seem to be repeated. However some visions we experienced together. My whole life in Christ began around a campfire after I left home and began living in a hippie camp. I hope you like reading how our lives were led by the Lord Jesus Christ.

The fire burned slower now as the crowd, tired, disappeared into tents or into the dark woods. I hadn't lived amongst the hippies for very long, just months since I'd left home. I was beginning to get used to the general routine of vacating the woods throughout the day and, by night, seeking a safe place to sleep. I sat staring at the flames as a guy, no more than twenty years old, gently prodded the log, causing the flames to jump a little and then settle back down. There were about five or six of us left up, not willing to give into the sleep that called us. One of the girls touched a cup that had been left to close to the heat, and as she yelped, she exclaimed, "Oh God."

That initiated a gentle conversation about the existence of God. The fire poker guy spoke first: "No such thing."

The girl answered him with a snicker and said, "Oh yeah, I believe there is."

A bright and funny young girl grew serious with a "There has to be something out there, but is it a god?"

I had no opinion, for in all of my fourteen years, I hadn't remembered hearing the term *God*. Mother had mentioned Jesus, but religion hadn't been that big in our house. I wondered about it now. Was there something powerful that existed somewhere? Perhaps watching, as my mother had indicated about Jesus. What exactly was a god, and what did a god do? I wondered about it so much that I decided to investigate, and the only thing I could think to do was to visit a church to see for myself. The campfire circle talked a little more about the universe and the earth not being the only place with life and that led to a conversation of aliens. I didn't care for the conversation, but I didn't want to lie on the ground with a dirty blanket either, even if the weather in Tampa was at an optimum temperature. Since I didn't have a tent of my own, the left-behind blanket was all that was available. Soon enough, the fire poker stirred the embers and headed to his tent. The stalling drew to an end, and I found the most private and safe spot. Many there were underage and probably runaways, myself ranking the youngest at age fourteen. No one shared too much information about themselves. The camp had people coming and going. Tents went up and came down. Sometimes you met people and never saw them again.

God kept coming to my mind, but I didn't bring it up to anyone. I met a girl named Charlotte from DC and she and I would panhandle together downtown. It was nice to have a friend to go places with.

Life went on that way for a while. Sometimes we would crash on Clearwater beach. It was really nice there, with the wind blowing and the water crashing on the beach.

I decided to go to a church to begin the investigation. The music and singing hit my ears as I opened the big heavy doors, and my eyes widened at the blood-red carpet. The music and singing ended as I entered. People started taking a seat. I noticed people stealing glances my way which prompted the selection of the seat closest to the door. The stares made me really uncomfortable. I couldn't blame them for wanting to stare because of the clothes that I had on, which included a tank top with a marijuana leaf on the front and bell-bottom pants. I was barefoot, except for foot jewelry. My hair was long and thin, to the waist, and an array of beads hung from my ears and around my neck.

The preacher began to speak, and I listened intently for the answer to my quest. "If God is real, where could I find him?" But he never said. At the end, he did an altar call. I didn't know what an altar call was at the time, but I felt the urge to run to the front. A few others stood and started down the aisle.

From where I was seated the altar was down below all the pews. I stood up and hesitated because I was embarrassed yet felt desperate to go. Descending the steps, I began going faster, throwing myself down on the floor in front of the altar. I cried hard, not knowing why. I wasn't praying or talking to God; I was just crying. Crying so hard, I was gasping for air. I sat up on my knees and back on my feet. A woman stood to my right, standing as far from me as she could and still be able to touch me with one finger. She asked me if I felt better. I was puzzled but nodded yes. Of course I did; I had just cried my heart out. I was lonely inside, and at that moment, I wished my mother had been there to hold me and hug me like she always had done. I missed her then.

The woman thrust a white card in my hand, and I got excited to think that this card would hold the secret to where God was and how I could see him. I was disappointed to read that I should fill out the card with name and address since now I was saved, and I could join the church. The woman told me to fill it out and drop it in the plate. She turned then and disappeared into the crowd. I tore up the card and watched the tiny pieces litter the blood-red carpet. I left and decided that God didn't live there, so I would go somewhere else the following Sunday. I didn't realize until years later that what had happened to me on the blood red carpet was *John 14:17 (KJV)*, "Even the Spirit of truth, whom the world cannot receive, because it see him not, neither know him; but you know him for he dwells *with* you, and *shall be in* you."

Jesus had sent the spirit because he had heard my heart. The Holy Ghost had indeed come to walk *with* me, but he was *not yet in me*. This is what happens when most people ask Jesus to come into their hearts (which is not biblical). They are told by the church that they are saved, but that isn't true. What happens at that point is that the Holy Ghost stays beside you, he is *with you* to bring you to a place of receiving him. Then when you are in the right frame of "heart" and you seek him further, he enters in. I left that church, disappointed; however, I vowed to continue my search, by going to a different denomination every Sunday.

Each church, it seemed, was a religion within itself, for they all had their own rules and their own beliefs.

"But in vain do they worship me teaching for doctrines, the commandments of men" (Matt. 15:9 KJV).

At each church, I was stared upon and treated as though I had a disease. No one would speak to me. One woman did approach me at a Church of the Nazarene. She held out a limp hand to me and with a forced smile on her face, said, "Welcome." She had been impeccably dressed like Jackie Kennedy. Pillbox hat on her sixties-styled hair and Jackie-styled skirt suit. I watched all these people and under-stood what the hippies called *plastic people*. They seemed to be acting in a play. After that, I determined "there is no God."

I met a biker called Churchkey and became a part of his world. This meant riding in a motorcycle club (like Hells Angels). This way of life was so opposite from the hippies, nothing of love and peace but of war and fierce rebellion.

They partied more, and they partied harder. This was a prelude of the hell that I was rushing to. One day, three of us pulled into a "head shop" parking lot. There was a group of young people in a huddle. The girl with me and her boyfriend got out of the pickup truck real quick. She hit her mouth on the side mirror, and blood trickled down her chin. One of the young men in the huddle, who was clearly older than our sixteen-year-old selves, approached her. He held her cut chin, and she winced. He said, "May I pray for you?" She just nodded. He put his finger right on the cut and said, "In the name of Jesus." He pulled his finger away. I audibly gasped because the cut was totally gone. The guy wiped the remaining blood from her chin and told her never to forget that Jesus loved her and maybe some other stuff, but I was still in awe of what I had seen.

After getting pregnant, Churchkey and I decided to get mar-ried with a biker wedding. Later, we were released by the hand of God from the club, and we moved to Charlotte, North Carolina. We didn't know you shouldn't move so far away when you are eight months along.

When we arrived in NC, I was feeling awful, and Churchkey took me to the hospital. I was admitted for observation with an over-night stay. I was nutritionally dehydrated, and the next morning, Churchkey showed up at my bedside. He sheepishly asked me if they could keep me another day. He then told me that he was out of money, and we had nowhere to go. After I was discharged, we sat in the waiting room, and he tried to think of what to do. Since I had never been in Charlotte before, I could not make a suggestion. He suddenly jumped up and announced that he could call the parents of a childhood friend. Then he added some dreaded words. "I know that they will let us stay a couple of weeks because the woman is a

Christian." I was shocked, and I wanted to scream out, "Noooooooo, not a Christian!" I had gotten my belly full of those people. As a biker's wife, it was not for me to argue against him. However, I did make my feelings known.

Mr. and Mrs. Roddy were nice people. She was a very different Christian from the ones that I had experienced. She prayed all through the day while she cooked and cleaned. She sang praises to Jesus and hummed melodies of happiness. I knew that God was real, and he was in this lady. They had a paralyzed son named Mike, and he had the bedroom by the back door. Everyone used the backdoor coming and going. One night, Churchkey fell in the back door and ended up in Mike's room. He had been drinking. He and Mike were talking. I could hear muffled voices, and then I heard Churchkey speaking in tongues. He had received. I was not happy for him. I felt betrayed. He had crossed over to their side without me. I was tremendously jealous.

I felt alone. I didn't really understand what had happened, but I knew he was like them now. He left each day and went to his new job while I watched Mrs. Roddy and I spent hours talking with Mike. I wanted what they had, even more then. Mrs. Roddy had a friend named Donna who came over a lot, and they would pray with Mike. I refused their invitations to pray, but in my room (where I would run to when I saw Donna at the door), I envied their happiness, and I asked God to give to me what they had.

After a week of listening to them pray and seeing God in them, my heart softened. I still didn't want to pray openly with anyone. I felt I'd make a fool of myself. In my room at night, I tried to make deals with God. "God, I know you're real. I felt you today and I can see you in them. They are holy and are for real, and I want you too, but I want it just between you and me." Immediately, I knew that you couldn't keep it secret, and yes, I would have to pray with them. "Okay, God, the next time they ask me to pray, I will." The next day, Donna came. I did not see her coming, or I probably would have run. My heart began to pound, remembering my oath. Well, they don't know about it, I reasoned, and I relaxed a little. It was short-lived because then, I had a thought, *God knew*. I slid forward on my chair in anticipation. They were talking as Donna came in, saying since Mike was asleep, they would pray there in the living room (where I was sitting). Donna greeted me, and they went straight to the sofa and knelt. They began to pray by saying, "Jesus, Jesus." I screamed within my mind, *What? They aren't going to asked me to pray?!* I felt relieved and afraid at the same time. Then I saw something very vivid in the darkness of my mind.

When I was still at home, I had a bumper sticker once that read "It's now or never" (it was in honor of Elvis's hit song). I saw it at that moment and its green letters were flashing like a neon sign. I knew this was it, my last chance! Without further thought, I jumped up and wedged my big pregnant self between them. The tears were there as soon as my knees touched the floor. They sang out praises in their surprise. Donna said to me, "If you want Jesus, lift your hands and praise him." My hands shot up, and through tears, I sputtered, "I praise you, Jesus!" I said his name over and over, faster and faster. I felt something filling me up inside, and something leaving me at the same time. The something leaving me was moving up from my feet, all the way up my body. When it got to my throat, it stopped as though it were stuck. There was a lump in my throat, like you get when you want to cry and hold it back. Through Donna, I heard the Holy Ghost say (it was her voice and his words), "See that devil run!"

I opened my eyes, and from right in front of my eyes, a gray fog moved away from me. It went through the window I faced and out into the yard. It wavered back and forth then disappeared. Before it vanished, I got a good look at it. It was in the shape of a person, but it had no face. It had no legs but looked like flowing clouds when it moved. I could see through it.

It reminded me of looking through gas fumes. When it disappeared, gladness came over me. My mouth stretched out in a big grin. My teeth began to chatter. A hum started from deep inside of me. Then my tongue got in on it; it pressed up to my teeth so that altogether it sounded like bees humming. "Oh! Praise God! Sense I believed, I now received the Holy Ghost and I was speaking in an unknown tongue!" (Acts 19). Speaking in tongues is praying 'in the spirit' and this is needed in order to worship.

"God is a spirit and they that worship him must worship him in spirit and in truth" (John 4:24 KJV). I didn't know that would happen, didn't know it could. I'm so glad I didn't miss my last chance. I felt clean and free from sin. My husband was called Churchkey by the club because he opened a bottle and a can with his teeth once. Now I knew he had been used by God as a key to the true church of Jesus for us to receive. Being possessed by a demon doesn't normally make you feel different; although it can alter personalities slowly over time. Demons influence behaviors and cause you to view things differently. Not everyone will see their demon leave, but the demons will leave when they call on Jesus. You may not think you have a demon because, after all, you are a good person and wouldn't hurt anyone. You don't have to have your head spinning, hiss at a cross, throw a Bible or be hateful, to be filled with a demon. Demons are influencing spirits or souls, not having a body. They are not fallen angels. They do not force you to sin. The devil cannot make you "*do it.*" Disembodied souls seek to inhabit a body. Demons influence all manner of sin. They slip in as you sin and help you to continue. There are no set criteria for a demon to possess someone except for the person to give in to a temptation and to have it in their heart because they enjoy the sin. What we read in the Bible happens now, for we are still living the Bible. Matthew 12, beginning with verse 43, shows you the characteristics of an unclean spirit. The unclean spirit can walk. They can look for (can see). The unclean spirit can speak. They can decide and strategize, plot and plan together. The unclean spirit wants to possess you because they want to use your body to sin with. They want to use your eyes to see clearly this realm and your hands to feel this world again. When you sin, they get the pleasure and you get the misery of it.

After we left Mrs. Roddys, we lived in a small mobile home not far down the street. I went through a trial immediately. I was tempted with cigarettes as I had quit before I received. I fought it off with prayer and resistance to the temptation by saying no with determination. I didn't have any problem with initiating the tongues. I have heard people say that they spoke in tongues when they first received but never had again. If I prayed and the tongues didn't come on their own, I would just repeat what I had done to receive, and I would start to speak in tongues before long. I've listened to music that moved me to tears or even watched a movie that had a part that made me cry deeply, and I'd get up and go pray with that emotion. Stir the emotion and you stir the spirit. I've been asked if I am doing it or if it happens by itself. The Bible says in Acts 2:4 (KJV), "As the spirit gave utterance."

In those early days, I just said his name over and over faster and faster. It comes on its own. I am not doing it. It feels the same as when you are out in the cold and your teeth begin to voluntarily chatter, and for some reason, we hum with it.

Two weeks after we left the Roddy home, I went into labor. The Holy Ghost got the stronger with each contraction. When we got to the hospital, there was no time for prepping or anything for pain. I didn't feel the pain so bad because the spirit was praying through me, and numbness went over the lower part of me. A nurse leaned over and asked me what I had said, and I answered her in tongues. She just patted my hand and kept telling me everything was good.

As soon as "Tommy Jr." was born, the numbness went away, and the Holy Ghost was quiet. I could feel calm in me. The day to leave the hospital brought a snowstorm, and I couldn't imagine leaving in that blizzard. I was used to Florida weather. So Churchkey called Mr. Roddy (since he drove a long-distance truck) and he and Mrs. Roddy drove us home.

I was so happy; I couldn't believe that I had a son. A child to love and would love me. Someone needed me as much as I needed him. He slept in a dresser drawer, and I was a confident young mother. I used cloth diapers, and he drank diluted carnation evaporated milk. The doctor said that was okay and that I should put Poly-Vi baby vitamins in a bottle per day and a few drops of Karo syrup if he was constipated. I prayed all the time and devoured the scriptures as though I had but a short time to read every word. The scriptures came alive for me as I learned of Jesus and his life on earth. The Word brought me closer to him than I could have imagined.

I had received the Holy Ghost in November. The following January, Mrs. Roddy and Donna came out to the country where we had moved to a larger mobile home park. It was snowing, and I rushed them in. After a few minutes, they said that they had come to baptize me. I asked them where we would go to be baptized. Donna spoke first, "We saw a small creek down the road." Really?

Were they crazy? It was freezing outside! They seemed matter of fact. They said it was necessary, so I got ready with lots of towels.

We trekked down a small hill and approached the creek bank. All I could see was the half-frozen water. I tried to not think about me going into that water. The stream looked too shallow, but Donna took my hand, and we helped each other down the creek bank. We laughed as we slipped and slid. Donna went straight into the water and motioned me to hurry in; she had been called by God to preach and to baptize in the name of Jesus. She laid me down in the creek water, and it wasn't that cold because it was over so fast. She had me wrapped in a towel before I knew it, and then I felt the cold. The cold isn't the only thing that I felt. I felt an awesome happiness, almost giddiness. Donna and Mrs. Roddy came again one day and while we prayed in unison. We were all huddled in the small living room. I had felt Donna moving, and I thought she was moving toward Mother (as she was behind me and unfilled), so I moved out of her way, but as I moved, I opened my eyes and I noticed that Donna's eyes were closed tight. She didn't move toward Mother, though, and with out-stretched arms, moved to follow me. When her hands touched me, the Lord spoke; He said, "I ordain you to preach and baptize in my name." When we had stopped praying, Donna said, "Now you can baptize Tommy" (Churchkey). That made me nervous. How does one perform a baptism? Even though I had been baptized, I hadn't paid much attention to how Donna had gone about it. It wasn't too long before they came back to witness Churchkey's baptism. It was still winter, so we faced the cold stream once again. Churchkey slid down the bank and helped me down too. I was shaking but not from the cold. Churchkey was five feet eight. I was five feet. I put my right hand to the back of his head and like someone not thinking, I put my left hand on his forehead. I said, "I baptize you in the name of Jesus." Suddenly he went backward. I had not initiated this, yet he was falling. I had no time to respond as I was like frozen to him. He was in the water before I knew it. He had gone straight backward; his body didn't bend. I could only hold onto him, and now as he was lying there under the water; it seemed as though he were dead—his skin was an ashen pale. I noticed that one air bubble escaped a nostril. Just as I saw that bubble, he rose out of the water, and all I could do was hang on. Straight as a board, he came out of the water. He took a deep breath, and Donna tossed us a towel. In the days that followed, I replayed it in my mind over and over and realized that the Holy Ghost had to have done it for me because there was no way I could have taken him down and back up with the way I was only holding his head. He had said later that he had planned to kneel but went into the water before he could.

Soon after this, my mother's live-in boyfriend died. She brought my brother Powell, who was thirteen and my sister, Cynthia, who was twelve at the time to stay with us. I was eighteen at the time. Mother and my dad had gotten divorced when I was nine. She had been living with Eddie for several years. Now he was gone, and Powell and Cynthia would be with me for a few weeks.

Churchkey prayed with me in the beginning, and we read the Bible together. Then he was gone most of the time. When he wasn't at work, he was with his old friends. I enjoyed the company of my younger siblings. They didn't have much to say, but they did listen to me when I told them of Jesus and how I received his spirit. I told them they could receive the same thing right then. They followed me to the bedroom where I thought they would feel more private. Beside the bed, they lifted their hands and began to say "Jesus." Powell started to utter a sound, but he caught himself and stopped the entry of the Holy Ghost. I asked him was he giving up and he said, "Maybe later." He then got up and left the room. The front door opened and closed again. He has not to this day in 2021 received the Holy Ghost. I turned to Cynthia who was silently crying. I asked her, "What about you? Are you going to quit?" She shook her head no and began to call out loudly the name of Jesus. She did so for a few minutes and then stopped and was sniffing. Cynthia stood up and went to the bathroom. I followed her and entered as the door was left open. She was blowing her nose.

"Well?" I asked, and she said very sweetly but firmly, "No, I'm not giving up!" She went to her knees beside the tub and lifted up her hands straight up and began to say "Jesus" over and over, faster and faster. Within seconds, she was speaking in tongues. The unknown tongue! It is the voice of the wind (spirit) as described by Jesus to Nicodemus in John 3:8. It is the tongue that Paul says he is glad that he speaks in more than them all (1 Cor. 14:18); it is the same tongue that Paul talks about in 1 Corinthians 13:1. He (Paul) says that he spoke in the tongues of angels (unknown tongues) and the tongues of men (earth languages) that if he didn't have love, though, it would be for nothing.

It is the tongues that are spoken of in 1 Corinthians 14:2, which say, "For he that speaketh in an unknown tongue speaketh not unto men, but unto God, for no man understandeth him, howbeit in the spirit he speaketh mysteries." The "lalalas" and the "dededees" actually is a language. It is sad that many charismatics and apostolic have been deceived to think that they have and can receive the Holy Ghost by determining within themselves that they have the spirit and just babble anything that comes to mind. It reminds me of someone just pretending to speak…say, French. No lessons just an idea of the sound. Go ahead pick a language and just pretend that you can speak it. LOL. You cannot receive the Holy Ghost (Spirit) through the head. It is emotionally sought. It is through the heart and not the head.

One night, Cynthia and I were sitting at the kitchen table of the small mobile home. We read the Bible, and we prayed a lot while they were with me. She devoured the scriptures as I had done, and we laughed so much, we cried. Powell still avoided all conversation that involved Jesus. He would be leaving in a few days. I think he would have come around if he could have been there longer. Everyone is free to choose.

Anyway, Cynthia and I sat there, and I kept wiping my hands because they were so oily, and then I noticed that as I wiped the oil off, more would pool up in my palm. It continued for hours. I was so young in the Lord that I didn't realize that he was anointing my hands for his work. An anointing is an appointment to office, not power but authority. We thoroughly loved being together.

One night, I was awakened by the sound of a strong wind. I thought that there was a terrible storm on us. The wind swirled around the trailer as though we were in the center of a tornado. It was so loud that I yelled for Churchkey to wake up. He was wide-eyed when he woke. "There's a storm," I yelled. He listened and shook his head, looking very puzzled. I said, "Don't you hear the wind?" He shook his head no and said, "Stop yelling before you wake the baby." He lay back down, and I thought something must be wrong with him. I went to get Cynthia; she would hear it, and I was sure. She was on the sofa, sound asleep. I shook her none too easy and was saying, "Do you hear it? Do you hear it?" Her answer was the same as Churchkey. She looked at me as though I had lost my mind, said no, and turned to go back to sleep. I was left awake and alone, trying to figure out why the wind was whipping around our house. After a few days, I realized it had been spiritual; what did it mean? I prayed and prayed, but the answer didn't come. I knew it was the Holy Ghost, but why? Acts 2 was my only clue. Soon it was time for Cynthia and Powell to leave. Not long after they left, Churchkey told me that I could live "this Jesus thing" but he couldn't do it. I was devastated. I had noticed that he was gone out more and more, and that when he came home, he smelled more and more of alcohol. From that point on, I didn't share anything spiritual, with him keeping it all to myself. I missed Cynthia after she left.

When Tommy was three months old, we moved back to Tampa, Florida. With a small van all packed up, we stopped at a phone booth so I could call Mrs. Roddy and Donna to say goodbye. Churchkey, as usual, was not prepared for a journey. When we got to Georgia, little Tommy was sick with a high fever. I had hoped it was teething, but he had an upper respiratory infection. We had to see a small-town doctor and get medicine, so that took almost all of the money. There would not be enough to make it to Tampa. I began to pray and hardly stopped. The van kept going.

After arriving, we stayed with my in-laws until we rented a small house on the river. Life went on there as it had in Charlotte, but without my prayer partners, Mrs. Roddy and Donna I was quite lonely.

Churchkey led his life and was gone most of the time. I read more Word and prayed even more. Not long after we got back to Tampa, Churchkey took me to my older sister's house in Lakeland and dropped me off for the weekend. Her husband Howard was gone fishing for the weekend. I was really nervous about telling Maranda about my having received the Holy Ghost. I guess the reason we are hesitant to talk about our experience is because it is not accepted nor practiced among mainstream denominations. When I received, my family and friends thought that I was crazy, and yours will do the same. Mainstream denominations teach that when one repents, they receive the Holy Ghost (the spirit) into their heart. This is not true according to the Bible. When one repents, we do so with our conscious will.

When we receive the Holy Ghost, we do so with our emotions, for we are yelling out his name in desperation and the tears are flowing. Repenting produces *John 14:17*. In the verses 15–22, Jesus tells the disciples that he is going to the father, but he isn't going to leave them alone. He will pray to the father, that he will send "another" comforter. This other comforter is the Holy Ghost or Holy Spirit. Both terms are used in the scriptures.

Jesus tells them that they know *him* (Holy Ghost) because *he* (Holy Ghost) had been *with them* and soon *would be in them*. In *Acts 2:2*, the Holy Ghost enters into them and they begin to speak in the tongue of angels. After this, they were empowered to do the same as Jesus. This is when they were born again.

In *John 3:8*, Jesus says this: The wind blows where it will and you can hear its sound but cannot tell whether it's coming or going, so is everyone who is born the second time or is born again (paraphrased).

The word *wind* is often used to describe the spirit. We cannot see the spirit, but when he comes, we will hear his voice. In *Acts 2*, the wind filled the house, and they were filled and spoke in unknown tongues. Maranda and I spent several hours together before I got the courage to approach her about Jesus. She had gotten baptized at nine years old, remembered going to church with Mother and Daddy, and now she felt she was all right with the Lord. I filled her in about what my life had been like for the past few years. I then continued with my venture to North Carolina and being filled with the Holy Ghost. She became agitated as she was making Kool-Aid and cleaned the kitchen over and over. I followed her room to room as she cleaned, picked up, and put away. I followed behind her with the Bible open and talking nonstop. In the early evening, we put my son and her three children down for the night. We went to the family room and sat down. I felt I had read all that I could and told her all I knew. So I asked if she would join me in prayer. She shook her head no. I knelt beside the sofa and I prayed mostly "in the spirit" (in tongues). After a few minutes, I turned and saw that she was crying. I asked her if she wanted me to pray for her. She shook her head yes. I walked behind the rocking chair and put a hand on her shoulder. I began to pray for her to receive. Suddenly she jumped up and started jumping around.

As she jumped around, she was clapping her hands and spoke in tongues. We grew close as we talked and talked about the Holy Ghost and we prayed and prayed. The next night, Saturday, we had gotten the kids down to bed, and we could hardly wait to pray again. In Maranda's darkened bedroom, very little light showing through the closed blinds. We paused in praying to blow our noses, for we cried throughout. I was still on my knees while she was sitting on the side of the bed. She glanced at me and gasped. "You're glowing!" she exclaimed. Looking up, I noticed that she was also glowing. I could hardly believe my eyes. It was as though a light bulb was on inside her body. We both went to the mirror to look at ourselves. I rolled up my sleeves to see if my arms glowed as well. They did, and I flailed them about. We laughed and praised the Lord. We prayed more. The next day, I had to leave her. We neither wanted to be apart, but we had no choice. I didn't see her very much, but when we could get together, we had the best time in the Lord.

Getting together meant praying. Oh, we did a little small talk, exchanged crochet patterns, and recipes. We read the Bible together. She quit smoking right after she received the Holy Ghost. She began to see angels and have other spiritual experiences. One weekend that I went to her house was an exceptional visit. She told me how she had prayed for the Lord to fill her home with angels, and he did. After she told me about it, I said, "How wonderful!"

She said, "No, it isn't either. Every corner I turn there is an angel, and I'm constantly startled. If I wake in the night, there would be one laying over me from head to toe. I want you to help pray that I won't see them, but I want them to still be here." I couldn't understand how anyone would want angels to leave, but I said nothing. The children had been put down to bed. I announced that I was thirsty and went for the kitchen.

She asked me to pop into the boy's room and check on their sleep status. As I turned the corner in the kitchen for the adjacent room, an angel rushed past me pushing against my leg. I felt the push and the wind it caused, and when I felt it, I looked down and saw a flash of light. I suddenly got goose bumps and tears filled my eyes. I ran to the living room visibly shaken with my tale.

My sweet sister said, "See, I told you." So we prayed that the angels would not make themselves known to her in that house but would keep their place. She didn't see them again there. Later, she would say that she regretted that prayer. Her husband had gone on a fishing trip for the whole weekend, so we had a couple of days to be together. Back at home, I began to grow sad and hopeless. Churchkey was running around on me and keeping company with a lot of x-club members. I decided that leaving was my only option. Churchkey had always been a bully, and he beat me. I was tired of him and his abuse. I spoke with my mother who lived in Maryland. She would send a ticket to the Lakeland, Florida, bus station. All I would have to do was to go to my sister's and then to the bus station. I was afraid of what Churchkey would do if I faced him. I felt the only way was to run.

The next month, when Mother would receive her pension check, I could go. I went to Maranda's a few days early so that I could be with her a little longer. I didn't want to leave her, but staying at their home was out of the question because of her husband. Her husband was out of town when I got there, and for two days, we had great prayer together. The Lord gave a message. The Lord uses me in this way…a lot. I will pray in tongues and then the Lord will interpret in English (as that is my language). The Lord told us, through me, that we would go on a three-day journey and that we would walk in his foot*prints*. The next day, Maranda's husband came home and told me to leave, in his usual hateful way by throwing little Tommy's stroller and my small suitcase out the front door and screamed for us to get out. Without ever saying hello or asking "What are you doing here?" he ordered me to leave. Maranda was begging him to stop doing this, and he screamed at her to go with me if she didn't like it.

She was crying, and I was telling her to stay and not go with me, but she packed a small case. I couldn't see her leaving her four children. She whispered to me that the kids would be okay and that she would come back. She knew it was days yet before Mother could buy the ticket, and she was afraid for me and little Tommy out on the streets alone. So we left then and we both were crying as I put Tommy in his stroller. We walked toward town with nowhere to go. It was a hot day in June. We started praying in tongues as we held one another's hand. She and I had never been close until we were both born into God's kingdom. Now we loved each other dearly.

The heat had gotten to us so we went to the bus station, and after informing the clerk that a ticket would be coming soon, we took a seat and just sat for a while. We didn't know exactly what to do. We had no car or money, not even change. We went to the lake in the center of town and let Tommy walk around since he had napped in the bus station. While we sat in the shade, listening to our stomachs growl, I came up with what I thought was a clever idea. We could call churches and ask for help. From a gas station, we used the phone. We called church after church and was turned down by them all. They didn't have a program to help homeless or hungry, even if a child *was* involved. So we prayed to know what to do. We went back to walking around. We spent all day the first day wandering. We went from bus station to streets to bus station. We walked around the town eating oranges and grapefruit that hung from the trees that were in people's yards. However, we never went into someone's yard and would only eat if the branches were hanging over into the alley.

We picked up pop (soda) bottles to cash in. They were five cents for each glass bottle returned. We needed ten cents to put in a pay phone to get the long-distance operator to place a collect call to Mother. The Spanish section was just ahead of us. When we arrived, we saw a few stores with a canvas cover over the store front. It was cool there with a nice breeze blowing. The empty bench in front of the plate glass window sure looked inviting. Maranda sat there with the empty stroller while I went in carrying Tommy on my hip. The air-conditioning sure felt good, and Tommy's little red and sweaty face could sure use some cool air. The lady at the counter grew suspicious of me because I wasn't buying anything and was just lingering, looking at different items. I smiled at her as I exited and sat on the bench. I told my sister about it, and she opted not to go in. She said the cool air would only make her more miserable when she faced the heat again. I was feeling frustrated because we needed another nickel. I leaned over and put my elbows on my knees, hands on my face. There right between my feet was a beautiful dime. "Oh my, oh my!" I was exclaiming. My sister was saying, "What? What?" I just reached down and picked it up and held it up to her. We both jumped up and held each other and, at arm's length, jumping up and down.

You would have thought that we had found a hundred bucks. LOL. We headed back toward the bus station where we would call Mother collect. As we walked down the sidewalk, she grabbed my arm and pointed to the sidewalk. "Look!" she said. I looked but saw nothing. "Watch my feet," she said. I did and saw nothing. Then she said, "Watch under my foot as I take a step." I could see what looked like a faint outline of a footprint, and it looked a little indented into the concrete, but I could barely see it. She described it to me as she could see it perfectly. Perhaps the Lord had said it and intended it for her only. As we walked our feet went into the footprints of Jesus just like he had said.

We had thought that he meant like when you say, "That boy is walking in his daddy's footsteps, but Jesus meant it literally, in his foot*prints*. When we called Mother, she said she had called the "Salvation Army," and we could stay that night. We were so happy that we would have a shelter over our heads. The place was empty until a couple of girls who were fruit pickers came in. We witnessed about Jesus and receiving his spirit. One girl was receptive the other was skeptical. We answered their questions, and when they seemed to reject us, we spoke of their work in the orchards. They were friendly then, and we spoke no more of the Lord to them. The next morning, we were told by the Salvation Army that we could only stay one night. So we faced another day in the sun and prayed Mother would receive her check that day. We walked the alleys again and I ate more citrus. We had been fed at the Salvation Army that morning.

Even without morning sickness, the oatmeal was nauseating no matter how grateful we were for it. We turned different corners so we didn't walk in circles. Suddenly we noticed that we were at the back of a grocery store and there was a "Ruth's Salad" truck. "I'm gonna ask the man for food," and of course, my sister protested. She wasn't accustomed to begging but having been a hippie, and panhandling on the streets, I had no pride. I left her and Tommy up the hill on the alley. I saw the man about to go into the store so I ran to him. I explained that we were on the streets for days while we waited for the bus ticket. The man pulled out so much food for us. He went in the store and got plastic spoons and bread. We have never forgotten that man. We know he will be rewarded. We couldn't take any of it with us because it was ninety degrees, it would surely spoil quickly.

He was so kind. He told us to eat all we wanted and to just leave the rest there on the delivery dock. He would take care of it. It began to get dark, so we went to the bus station to see if the ticket had come. The man said that Mother had called and left a message for us to go back to Salvation Army; they would let us stay another night. We quickly obeyed. The bus station closed at 8:00 p.m. Lakeland was a small town then. The next day, the tickets arrived, and we made our way to Baltimore, Maryland. I told Maranda that she didn't have to go with me, but she would not leave me and Tommy alone. When we boarded the bus, I could only think of sleeping. Suddenly, my sister nudged me and pointed outside the bus window. I looked and saw what looked like a thin cloud, but she told me she could clearly see an angel going with us. In Baltimore, we enjoyed our mother and siblings. After two days, I began to have some cramping and became concerned for the baby. Mother took me to the hospital. I had not been seen by a doctor and had not been told by a doctor that I was pregnant, only the spirit had told me. When an Asian doctor came in, she asked me why was I there and I told her, "I'm pregnant and have some cramping." She said, "Who told you? You are baby." Her English was very bad.

I told her, "My Lord Jesus."

She said, "Who is that?"

I said, "My God. She shook her head and raised her hands in a question. After examining me, she told me I was indeed with child. I was two months along. The Lord is always proving himself to us. It wasn't long, and Churchkey hunted me down and forced me to go with him. He moved us then to North Carolina.

I made the most of my situation and did my wifely and motherly duties. Jesus was my refuge and my strength. Harley was born September 13, 1973.

"You are so beautiful," I had whispered, looking into his dark blue eyes. His tiny fist moved wildly about as though he were excited by my speaking to him. His hair was so full at his birth and now he looked odd with half of his head shaved. Tears trickled down my face as I spoke softly, words declaring my love for him. My mind raced back to my experience with Tommy. This had been so different.

I had given birth to Tommy with nothing for pain. No meds at all. It had been natural. The spirit had prayed through me the whole time of the quick birth. Afterward, they let me see him right away. Harley was different. Everything had been different. I didn't get to see him after his birth. They put me under after the first few pains. I woke up in a room with three other young women in their beds. They began to receive their babies for feeding. I said nothing, thinking they were waiting to bring my baby after I could go to the bathroom. I went and waited. No baby. Nurses came to retrieve the other women's babies. The last nurse was about to leave, and I raised the courage to ask her, "Miss, when will I see my baby?" She made a show of asking my name and told me she would inquire. Another nurse came in the room and walked right up to my bed. She had a serious look on her face. She came close, so no one else would hear. "The doctor would like to see you before you see your baby." My heart fell into my stomach. "Now?" I muttered. She shook her head as she reached for my blanket, turning it back and helping me to my feet.

In a small room at the end of the hall, a young man in a white coat sat writing and looking important. He didn't look up when I entered but did when he finished. "You are Beth Polson?" he had asked. His name was Dr. Goodman. He was an intern at the state hospital in Charlotte. He would be Harley's doctor. He began to tell me that they could not determine the sex of the baby as of yet. My mind was spiraling. What did he mean? Boy or girl, why could they not tell? I could hardly hear his words. He was telling me something about test and knowing for certain. Dazed, I went back to my room. Why did doctors have to be so non-feeling?

On the third day, I could go home; Harley had to stay. He was asleep now, and I ran my finger along his cheek, burning into my memory his face, his hair, eyes, even the little pucker of his lips as he fidgeted. He was going to die, this little baby. They had performed their test and determined that his urethra tube had deformed and twisted to be formed just under the scrotum, and there a urine slit had formed. He was all male. But that didn't make me jump for joy. I didn't know how long I had with him and no one, especially Dr. Goodman, believed me when I told them that he would die. I even witnessed to him and told him about how the prophecy came about. About how the day I had gotten out of the hospital, I had called one of my prayer partners.

This lady is used by the Lord to speak through, and I had sought her prayers in hope that the Lord would tell me something of my trouble. I walked to the phone booth, believing he would tell me everything would be okay. When she answered, I had said to her, "Please pray with me, about the baby. I don't want to say anything else, please pray." We prayed. The Holy Ghost spoke to me through her, saying, "Your baby will return unto its maker. Choose this day, whom you'll serve." My first thought was that God knew who I served, why did he say to "choose this day whom I would serve?" Then it hit me.

He also said my baby would return unto the maker. From that day, I prayed, not that he would change his mind and spare my child.

I didn't try to plead for my child's life. This is God and there would be reasons. I began to grieve but I would put off this feeling from time to time. I would bury it deep into my soul. Then I would pray, "Please don't let him die in my arms." A week would pass while my mind was in a blur. Dr. Goodman called me and my husband into the little cubicle of an office. "We can repair the baby's urethra and slowly over a period of a few years he will be just fine." I was totally confused. This wouldn't cause death. I didn't want to second guess God, but I couldn't help wondering that maybe he meant later in his life. Then one day the hospital called. Harley had suffered heart failure. He was two months old. All the way to the hospital, I cried and prayed, "Please help me through this."

Harley was on a respirator when we arrived. They had run more test and discovered that he had only one lung. His heart arteries were deformed. He had a heart valve that worked backward. His blood was not being distributed correctly throughout his body. "Dear God," I whispered, staring into the little closed in hospital equivalent of a bassinet. He had tubes and IVs going in and out of him, even in his head. "Please be merciful and don't let him suffer." Dr. Goodman came near, and when I turned to look at him, I saw in his eyes the remembrance of God's words of a prophecy. He held onto this realm of logic and hope and told me that Harley's condition had stabilized. He said that they would try to get him strong enough for surgery to fix his heart valves. I didn't say anything, but I know my tears sang my heartache. While all of this was taking place, my marriage was… well, it wasn't.

While I went to the hospital and saw our child, my husband continued in the wild life of drugs, drinking, other women, and partying with friends. No, it wasn't his way of dealing with a hurt, for he had never stopped this lifestyle. I always thought that when you got married, you stopped behaving like children and entered the world of responsibility and adulthood. It wasn't turning out that way. Even if I had not been enlightened to truth by the infilling of the Holy Spirit, I would have wanted to settle down and for us to be a family. I had God and my two-year-old Tommy, and my little sister Cynthia to hold onto to make it through this. If Cynthia had not been with me, I don't know how I would have made it. She was only fourteen, but she was so precious. Because she had received the Holy Ghost, we prayed together. Tommy on my lap mostly while our spirits prayed for the things we don't know anything about.

At the hospital, as I stood looking at Harley in the little hospital issued tee; I kept whispering into his ears, "I love you, precious." I wanted him to carry my love with him. So when I die, he will know me right away. He got strong enough for the surgery. Dr. Goodman told us that a famous heart surgeon from New York just happened to be in Charlotte and had volunteered to do Harley's surgery pro bono. We were already on social services. The march of dimes, the Shriner's and the state were picking up the hospital tab. I wanted to have hope that God would let him live, that my faith was a lie, or I had imagined the whole thing. I wanted this big shot Dr. to do his magic, work all of his talents on my little precious. In my deepest heart, I knew my God was real and that he still speaks to his own. I knew I had heard his word. We kissed Harley and walked away. The surgeon would do his thing and I asked God to bless him for his giving heart and for caring for our child. The wait was going to be a long one, they said.

Dr. Goodman called us to a meeting. "His only lung is on the side that we have to go in on. The surgery will last several hours. If he doesn't get too much bruising on his lung, he may have a chance. After the surgery, we'll watch him for signs of pneumonia. If he doesn't get pneumonia, he'll make it." He told us to go home, and they would call us. I couldn't leave. I was surprised, but Churchkey stayed at the hospital with me. The surgery over, Dr. Goodman told us everything went well. We would not be able to see him for a while.

We went home. In a few days, Harley seemed to be so much better. He was eating better and had more color in his cheeks. He was more alert and held onto my finger with a strong grip. He had been in the hospital for a little more than two months. One day, I went to see him and his crib was empty. I found him at the nurses' station with only a diaper and T-shirt on, being held by a nurse who was trying to work the desk. Harley's legs and arms were purplish. I went to take him from her (they all knew me by now) as a visitor leaned in and cooed in his face. It was obvious she had a cold.

Now in November, middle of winter, I hurried him to his room and bundled him in a blanket. I was surprised to see that three other children had been moved into the ward. Two of them had pneumonia, and the third had an upper respiratory infection. I was worried about Harley catching a cold. It had only been a week since his surgery. Soon the hospital called us and said that he could go home. I had to hunt down my husband and we went to bring him home. I prayed all the way there.

"Please, God, if you are going to take him, please not at home, not in my arms." We arrived with a set of clothes for taking him home and a friend gave me a new blanket. I dressed him and talked to him. My husband held him a bit while we waited for a release. I noticed that Harley wheezed some and his breathing was labored more than usual. Dr. Goodman and the resident doctor checked his breathing and listened to his chest, they decided to keep him a few more days. I went back to visit the next day to find him back on a respirator. "He has pneumonia." Dr. Goodman told me in a matter-of-fact way. "We're doing everything we can and he is holding his own for now." Again I go home and wonder, "When, God, When?" I was cleaning a house as a job when I had a sudden urge to call Mrs. Roddy's sister in Baltimore. I called collect. "Molly, please pray with me" We prayed briefly. The spirit spoke through her: "It is finished," the Lord said through her. I started crying so hard that I simply hung up the phone. I got up from my knees, walked from the bedroom to the kitchen. The phone rang. Everyone had the number in case of emergency. I could hardly speak. "Hello, hello." I gulped through the tears. My father-in-law said, "Little darlin' I guess you already know, he said. The hospital just called me." I couldn't talk only cried harder. He had supposed that the hospital had called me first. He was gone. My precious little son was gone. How could I live? How could life go on without him? Oh, how my heart hurt. God's word had come to pass.

Why? I cannot tell. God in his wisdom knows what is best for us. I may have been hurt worse if Harley had lived. He may have hurt worse. Only God knows. I was in a daze as the funeral progressed. Well-wishers, known and unknown, passed by me in a blur. I lived on and I loved the son I had living. Tommy will be forty-nine this year (2020). Harley would have been forty-seven this year. I had another son, Michael, and a daughter Brandy. They are forty-five and forty-four. Life can hurt us, but I have had more joy than pain. God has been so good to me. I think of Harley so often, and like now, as I write, I grieve, I cry, and I live on. God had warned me to choose whom I served. I could have denied the word God had given, or I could have blamed God and been angry with him for my pain, but I chose God that day and ever since that day in 1973. It had been a difficult year. I was two years old in Jesus. Losing Harley and Churchkey misbehaving like a wild teenager made me grow up a little more. I've since learned how not to be moved by the actions of others. Cynthia stayed with me a while longer. She and I had received the Holy Ghost only a few months apart, so we were both new to the ways of praying in the spirit. When Churchkey came in, we didn't pray or speak of heavenly things. However, he was hardly ever there so we did a lot of praying and Bible reading. The Lord was teaching us a lot and the prayer time we had was great. We exercised and had fun and it was good to laugh in the face of such heartache.

There were two stores near the house. One was almost next door, but it was closed down and even the phone in the booth was broken. So when we ever wanted to make a call, we would walk the extra block and use that phone booth.

That store was real busy, and it was well lit at night, all the way from our house to it. One night, about 10:00 p.m., the Lord spoke two complete sentences through me and one of them was to "go this minute and call your sister, tell her what I said." So we gathered up Tommy and walked to the furthest of the store's phone booth to call Maranda, who was still in Florida.

We were in the middle of the call when a young man in a hot rod-type car kept revving his engine. His car was parked right at the booth, and we were sure he could see us having difficulty hearing. So I motioned that we would be just another minute. Still, he revved his motor.

We hurried through the call, and as soon as we hung up the phone, he sped off with squealing tires. We began the walk home, and as we neared the closed-down store, we saw the same car parked by the broken phone booth. He was just standing there, pretending to talk on the broken phone. We laughed, knowing that he was up to something, and he didn't know that we knew the phone he was holding was broken. We usually would be cutting just beside that phone booth, but being leery of him, we walked to the far side of the parking lot. Just as we came even with the booth but still a safe distance away, he swung open the door very fast, which made us jump a little. He then jumped out of the booth and spun around. He had his pants undone and his hands were on his "privates." He twirled it around like a cowboy working a lasso and asked us if we wanted a good time. We both began quoting scripture and shamed him for his behavior. He quickly and with shame "put it back" with a shocked look on his face. He ran to his car and sped off without even closing the door. We were still yelling scripture when he hit the highway.

"What fruit had ye (you) then in those things whereof (of what) ye are now ashamed for the end of those things is death" (Rom. 6:21 KJV).

I have wondered about him. Did he change his life? We realized he was the real reason for the mission on which we had been sent. No matter what choice he made he had heard the word of God. Every ear shall hear the word of God. What they do with it is up to them. We were not ashamed to give this man God's Word.

"Whosoever therefore, shall be ashamed of me and of my words in this adulterous and sinful generation; of him also shall the son of man be ashamed, when he cometh in the glory of his father with the holy angels" (Mark 8:38 KJV).

When Tommy was five, Michael was two, and Brandy was a year old, we had yet moved to another place, a little house by Charlotte Douglas airport. I was holding a cup of coffee as I walked into our sunny living room. I stood in front of the big bay window for a moment before I noticed them standing there. My neighbor Lavinia, her mother, and her daughter were all three standing in their driveway, looking up at the sky. We had lived across the street from

Lavinia and her family for a year. Before we moved there, I had been praying about where to move to and all the Lord said was "You will see a yellow house." That first morning when I had awakened and stood up on the mattress that had been thrown on the floor the night before, under that same big window, there it was a big yellow house, Lavinia's. I knew that my husband had found and moved us into the right place. We had moved in while it was dark.

But now, as I stood there, I wondered to what they were looking. I went out on the front porch holding Brandy on my hip. As soon as Lavinia saw me, she motioned for me to come across the road. I did so as quickly as possible. They all three at once started telling me what they were seeing. "The sun has gone crazy," they were saying. Sandy, Lavinia's daughter took Brandy from my hip, so I could look at it unencumbered. I could hardly believe my eyes! The sun was in the process of splitting in two. It came apart in equal halves and then went back together like the blobs of a lava lamp. It then looked as though it had something silver right on top of it. We were all staring right at it, and it didn't hurt our eyes. It moved a few other ways as though to entertain us.

Only when it was completely still did I turn to leave. "Surely it will be on the news." I told them as I headed for the house. To my surprise, it wasn't. I was confused; surely everyone saw that, or at least someone other than just us. Of course there was no way to know in that day as there were no computers. No social media then. It had been amazing to see. In 2000, I got my first PC, and when YouTube began, I started seeing accounts of others having seen the sun acting odd. Brandy was three months old when we moved in front of the yellow house.

When I was nursing her, I would awake at every little sound, thinking it might be her ready to nurse. One night, I awoke when I heard her cry a little. The house was built around a small square hallway. From that hallway, you could enter into the two bedrooms, bath, kitchen, and living room. I had gotten up and was standing by the doorway leading to the kids' room. I waited, but Brandy didn't make another sound. I hadn't noticed the time, so I just leaned against the doorframe to wait. I could feel in my body that it was close to time.

As I dozed off, I heard my name loudly echoing throughout this little house with no carpet or rugs. I jerked up and tiptoed to my and Churchkey's room, thinking that it was he that had yelled. No, he was snoring. Mmmmm, I was puzzled but was too sleepy to contemplate it. The doorframe awaited my tired eyes. You know a sleepy mother with a newborn can sleep anywhere. As again I dozed, again I heard the loud voice say my name. I jerked up, and again I heard it! I was very awake this time, and at first, I thought it was Jesus calling me, so I said, "Here I am, Lord." That's what I had read in the Bible. Immediately I knew that it was not Jesus but an angel. With a loud and echoing sound, he spoke to me, "Pick up your Bible and read." His voice had lowered and softened when he said it.

Looking just inside the living room, I saw my Bible on the children's small chair. I had slipped it there before going to bed. The front porch light was on. The front door had three rectangle windows set in a cascading pattern. The light now shone from one of the windows and was a ray on the Bible like a deliberate spotlight. I reached for it while wiping tears to see. "You'll have to tell me what to read. You know that I don't understand much of this," I said through tears to him.

He then said, "Read Revelation 7, 'For this is the time in which you live and you have but one day.'" I flipped through the pages and read the chapter. "What does this mean?" I asked him, but there was no answer; he had gone. After a time, I did understand it. The 144,000 are being picked and sealed (marked). They are *Jews*, twelve thousand from each of the twelve tribes. They will be here after rapture to witness for Jesus against the anti-Christ. When he said I had but one day, I thought he meant a literal day! I discovered it to mean we were in the end of days or the last days. Now, in 2021 they *may* be already picked and sealed. The 144,000 are not Jehovah's Witness. They are not Mormons or any other Christian group. The second part of chapter 7 talks about the white throne judgment, which is everyone who is beheaded for Christ in the tribulation.

We moved to a mobile home park on the opposite side of Charlotte. We were always moving, it seemed. Mother came to stay with us for a while. She was still going to country music bars to drink and dance. She said that she got lonely, and she was just having fun and passing the time. One afternoon, she asked me some questions about Jesus.

I didn't have the answer to all of her questions, but I did my best. She had been watching me pray in tongues and worship openly, and she began to see that I was different. She always thought she had Jesus in her heart. Mother met Henry, the man next door, and they hit it off. She spent a lot of time with him, his son, and his son's wife. Bars no longer held her interest. One day she came to my door, and as she waited for me to sweep up trash and move the baby away from the door, she looked up into the sky and gasped. She said, "Oh, come out and look." It's a big pulpit and it has a huge book on it. It's a white book and the pages are turning. She was breathless. I got the baby up and stepped outside, but it was fading from view. "What was it, Beth?" We sat at the table and I explained the book of life and the plan of salvation, the true way to receive Jesus and the promise of the Father.

"Being assembled together with them, commanded them that they should not depart from Jerusalem, but wait for the promise of the Father, which, saith he, ye have heard of me" (Acts 1:4 KJV).

> And suddenly there came a sound from heaven as of a rushing mighty wind, and it filled all of the house where they were sitting.
> And there appeared unto them cloven tongues like as of fire, and it sat upon each of them.
> And they were all filled with the Holy Ghost, and began to speak with other tongues, as the Spirit gave them utterance. (Acts 2:2–4 KJV)

My mother was always innocent minded and naïve. "How do I do that, Beth?" she asked. I told her how to get on her knees and lift her hands up to God and praise Jesus. "Show me," she said excitedly.

I started to tell her again and she said, "No, no, do it yourself and show me." So I got down on the floor in front of the kitchen sink as that is where we were standing. I lifted my hands, and with great feeling, I began to say "Jesus" over and over. She said, "Okay, okay! I got it! Get up." So I got up, and she went to her knees. Mother was forty-two, and she was calling on Jesus to give her everything he had! She praised and praised. I had my hands on her and was praying for the spirit to fill her, but I could feel a block. I had the urge to fill a cup with water. I turned to the sink and filled a kiddy cup with water. I thought that the Lord might have her drink it, but as I was coming around with the cup, my hand jerked and water doused her head. She jerked and hollered out. I felt demons running and could feel the wind of them as they passed by me. She began to shake and her lips were stammering as though she were cold but no sound left her. She stopped and was exhilarated. I kept thinking, *But she didn't speak in tongues*. The scripture came to me: "For with stammering lips and another tongue will he speak to this people" (Isa. 28:11).

She did the same as I had. I sounded like a bee humming or like my teeth were chattering. She still trembled for some time after, and she kept saying how clean she was now. I was excited for her too, and we hugged and laughed.

Acts 2, Acts 10, and Acts 19 all show receiving and speaking in tongues. Chapter 8 of Acts shows us that even believing, repenting, and being baptized in Jesus's name does not necessarily bring the baptism of the Holy Ghost. The people had believed and were baptized still the Holy Ghost had not entered into.

Some people think the scripture below says that believers don't need a sign; however if the speaking in unknown tongues is a sign to nonbelievers, then doesn't it stand to reason that it is a believer doing the speaking in tongues? I think it was common place to the early church that speaking in tongues was a given when filled.

"Wherefore tongues are for a sign, not to them that believe, but to them that believe not: but prophesying serveth not for them that believe not, but for them which believe" (1 Cor. 14:22 KJV).

Speaking in tongues is a complicated subject for people with the Holy Ghost, so for people without, is almost impossible to comprehend.

Here is my understanding, though, and after a lot of study, I believe I am correct.

When we receive the Holy Ghost, the spirit will announce his arrival by praising Jesus as Jesus said he would do: "But when the Comforter is come, whom I will send unto you from the Father, even the Spirit of truth, which proceedeth from the Father, he shall testify of me" (John 15:26 KJV).

Anyone who goes to church will agree that when you are asked to "testify," you will more than likely stand and speak. Another example would be a person in court taking the stand to testify. That person will speak and tell. People think that kind of tongues is different Earth languages, but it isn't. This form of speaking in tongues is the language of heaven and no one on Earth understands it. This form is not a gift. It is the voice of the spirit. Some call it the initial sign of having received. In *Acts 2* after the disciples received the Holy Ghost, the people heard them speaking in at least sixteen different languages, and they may have begun to be used by the spirit after they left the upper room with the "gift of tongues," which is found of the nine spiritual gift of the spirit listed in *1 Corinthians 12*. The miracle of *Acts 2* is that the three thousand people *heard* their own language. It's my own opinion, mind you, that the disciples are speaking in the unknown tongues but the crowd heard their own language. The "gift of tongues are earth languages." The spirit will decide who to use which gift with. It isn't ours to have. I would not be able to say that I have knowledge and wisdom even though I had been used in that gift. The gift of tongues is Earth languages that the spirit may have you to speak in if he needs you to. It is not the unknown tongues also called the tongue of angels or the voice of the spirit, and there is interpretation of tongues in that list. This one allows you to understand a foreign (to you) Earth language. I imagine this can happen say if you are on a plane seated next to someone speaking Italian and you don't. The spirit may have you, who are spirit filled, tell this person about being filled. You speak in Italian, but to your own ears, you may only hear your language. And then the opposite of that, they speak and you hear your language. I truly believe that the Jews were speaking in an unknown tongue but that all of the sixteen nations "heard" their own language.

Mother asked me to come next door and explain to Henry and his son about this wonderful faith. I did, but you could feel the skepticism in the room. They didn't say anything against what I had shown them in the Bible or the words that I said, but they did not believe. One day, she burst into the house and said she had seen an angel. I was so excited to hear that. She had seen him behind her as she looked into the mirror. She and Henry had gotten married two weeks after they met and after a few months moved onto his thir-ty-three-foot cabin cruiser that was moored on Lake Gaston. Lake Gaston is on the North Carolina-Virginia state line. I went to visit her after a couple of weeks, and I baptized her there in a beautiful spot on the lake as the sun was setting. We were there with hands raised, both of us speaking in the tongue of angels.

"Though I speak with the tongues of men and of angels, and have not charity, I am become as sounding brass, or a tinkling cym-bal" (1 Cor. 13:1 KJV).

Simply said, even though I speak in my language and in the heavenly language, if I don't have love then it's all for nothing. Now my mother, myself, and my two sisters had received the gift of the Holy Ghost with the evidence of speaking in tongues as the spirit of God gives us utterance. We were all living apart from each other now. Mother was in Henderson, North Carolina. I was in Charlotte. Cynthia had gotten married and was living in Baltimore. Maranda and her husband had gotten ten acres of land in York, South Carolina, with hopes of building a house someday, but for the time being, they were living in a camper on the land. I had gotten strep throat, and Mother had come to take care of me and the kids. After I got well, we went down to see Maranda. Oh, how I had missed her. It was a hot and dry summer. It was June of '77. We arrived on a Friday after-noon, and Maranda's four children came spilling out of the camper, with flailing arms rushed to Mother's car. There was much laughter all around as the children were talking ninety miles a minute. My sister stood at the door, looking troubled but smiling in spite of it. We gave hugs to her as we entered the small space. Howard pushed past us with a scowl on his face and slammed the door behind him. I think I said before he hated all of her family, but especially me and Mother.

"What's wrong with him now?" I had to ask, already knowing the answer. She sighed. "Well, we have all weekend because he's gone fishing." We all knew fishing was just code for something else and he was probably glad we were there so he could bluster out. We had a good time catching up. We told all the news we each had since our last visit, and it had been years since we were all three together. As dusk appeared, we were all talked out and someone said, "Let's pray." Friday night was wonderful. We prayed way into the night. There were seven children all together. My sister's four, ages five to twelve, and my three, ages two, three, and six. I think that it is very interesting that my sister and I had four children each; we each had one girl and three boys. Her daughter came first, and mine came last. The children were scattered all around us on sofa and blankets on the floor. They eventually fell asleep where they sat. The children would pray, saying, "I praise you, Jesus." We had them to do this because this is how you seek to be filled with the Holy Ghost. We believe that prayer is praising God and worshiping him in spirit and truth.

"God is a spirit and they that worship him must worship him in spirit and in truth" (John 4:24 KJV).

The next morning, the children woke early. We pulled out eggs and pancake mix. The children began to be rowdy, so we sent them outside. They went to the back of the camper in the shade of the tall trees. It wasn't hot yet but could get that way in the sun. Suddenly, there was banging on the side of the camper, and we could hear some yelling. The stove was cut off, and the three of us was out the door to investigate. The children were all talking at once so my sister's older boy Robert told us what was wrong. "Mike thinks that's a devil." He was pointing to a water trail caused by the air-conditioning. "Oh," we sighed in relief as Maranda explained to him what the trails were and that the two points exited the round part wasn't a devil at all. Children's imaginations will take over at times if spiritual things are spoken of. Just then Robert shouted, "Look," and he pointed out over our heads to the sky. We followed his pointing finger and we were astonished to see a real casket. It was too far at first to see it good, and we guessed as to what it was, but it was moving closer. It also was turning as though on a turntable to display it for purchase. It stopped just over the trees and stopped spinning. It was a beautiful casket. It was a beautiful red mahogany with gold trim, and it gleamed. It had two sections as the head portion opened, and the casket tilted a little to show us who was inside. It was Maranda's husband, Howard. We had so many questions. Was Howard about to die? Did this mean he was dead spiritually and would never come in? Just then, the casket dissipated like I've seen clouds do.

This was not a cloud as there was not one cloud in the sky. Just as the casket disappeared, three men appeared to our left in the sky. They were only visible from the hips up. They were our husbands. They held hands and moved in a way that children do when playing ring-around-the-rosy. As they moved, they made hateful faces and had evil in their eyes. As they moved, there would always be one with his back to us but would turn the head to see us. Please understand that the images we saw moved and acted as real. The casket looked real and solid. The men looked real. Our husbands disappeared from the sky. Just as they did, we saw Howard appear, and he was holding a baby wrapped in a blue blanket. He was from the waist up only. He was looking down at this baby so endearing as though he loved it so much. Then he raised the baby at an angle to show us, and to our horror, it was a baby's body with Howard's adult head. Then he disappeared.

We thought the show was over, and we moved to the front of the camper to return to breakfast. We talked excitedly about what we had just seen. By this point, we weren't shocked by what we saw or experienced in the spirit because we had already seen and experienced much.

Yet we did get excited, and we praised him even more! Just because we had seen so much in the sky, we were still looking up and all over the sky with expectation and there it was; dark lines forming quickly as though some invisible hand with invisible charcoal were drawing something.

It was a tabby cat. Then suddenly the cat came to life and began to lick its coat. We were clapping and shouting praises! Then it disappeared just like the other images. Immediately, more charcoal lines and more images of animals of all kinds. He at one point just had like an oval window open and showed us African herd animals running across the plains. Then it all stopped, and there was a silence. Everything got very still, and I could hear the roar of the earth turning. I thought to myself that it is so loud why had I never heard it before? We waited and looked and then an angel appeared in the sky. Then another and another until the whole of the sky as far as we could see were filled with angels. They all looked alike. They had hair that was blond. It was cut with bangs and was the length of the chin. Their faces were strong and angular. Some had wings and some didn't. The ones without wings are the common angels and are in service to man. These are the ones that we may entertain unaware. Some were small and some were gigantic. There was a huge one with a tiny one in his hand. They had their hands out in front of them and lifted a little with their palms up. They didn't look at us but held their gaze to the heavens.

We had been holding onto each other and crying. It was so majestic, and we could feel the holiness. They had on what looked like light gray tunics almost to their knees and had leather-looking belts and shoe straps. We thought surely that would be the end but no, not so. Suddenly there was a huge angel in the sky. She stood with her hands on her hips and looked real stern. She was huge in the sky and then she walked across the sky in front of us. This one looked like a woman as the others looked like men soldiers. This one had long curly black hair that was billowing as though from a wind and wore many robes of silky layers. Part of the layers was outlined in brilliant red. Her face was stern looking with her eyebrows furrowed, and her expression was one of determination to perform her task. She came to a stop, and she slung her right arm down toward us, pointing a finger.

We all three gasped and held each other as we shrank back away from her. She then, in a hard motion, slung her, pointing right hand out toward the sky to our right.

There in the sky was a diadem, which is a thin crown. The crown was turning like the casket had done, moving as though on a display turntable. It then lifted up on one side so we could see the inner band. There on the inner band was the symbol of the Star of David.

Mother asked, "What does that mean?"

"I don't know for sure, but I think it means 'king of the Jews,'" I told her. We were all laughing now and praising God as it suddenly got dark, and we could see no more. The kids were all a clamor about what they had seen as we headed for the camper.

As we stepped into the camper, we began to laugh even harder because we saw the breakfast makings still on the table, and we realized that we all had been outside from about 8:00 a.m. until it had gotten dark. None of us, not even the kids, had gotten hungry, thirsty, or went to potty. So we all ate, very hardy, and another night, we praised him. The next day, Howard showed up about eleven. He didn't speak to us. He just walked over to my crochet basket (that I hauled everywhere I went) and threw it out the door. That was our cue to leave. We bid Maranda and the kids goodbye, and we left. In the next two years, we all three would be free and divorced from the ungodly husbands. In 1981, I met my second husband. We dated twice at family restaurants with the kids. After only a couple of weeks, he asked me to marry him. He was alone and didn't like it and he said that I would be providing a family and that he could provide support and stability. I said okay. I knew he was kind and gentle, and he accepted the way I lived my faith. I was also lonely and tired of the struggle. I had been hiding out for a long time and Junior (what I call my second husband) had an ex that was hounding him, so I suggested that we move out of the state so we could start new and fresh. Junior had a brother in the Panhandle of Texas. His brother gave us the okay to come out and we could stay for two weeks to get on our feet. So right after our nuptials at the York, South Carolina, courthouse, we packed up and headed for Wheeler Texas. I was twenty-eight and Junior, twenty-nine.

We know how those new settlers must have felt going west by wagon train; for the excitement we felt, I'm sure mirrored theirs. We were going to a new land and have new experiences. A brand-new life awaited us, and we eagerly drank in all of the scenery along the way. Going up the Appalachian Mountains toward Ashville, North Carolina, just an hour from Mooresville, our starting point, smoke came barreling out from under the hood of the '64 Plymouth valiant.

Highway I-40 was under construction on the steepest part and traffic was moving slower than normal. Good thing too because the little Plymouth was having a hard time on the upward climbs with its weight and the loaded down four-by-eight trailer behind it, and now smoke! Junior pulled to the center of the road, parking between two orange barrels. We both jumped out and looked under the hood. After the smoke cleared some, we saw the first aid box sitting on the motor. While packing for the trip, I had handed it to one of the kids to give to Junior. He was changing the oil and such and must have just taken it absent mindedly. After its removal, we laughed, relieved that it wasn't the car itself. We got as far as Arkansas the first night and had no money for a motel. We tried to sleep in the little car with the windows down because of the heat, but the mosquitoes worked hard at making a meal of us.

So before long, we were riding again. I saw the mountains in North Carolina and in Tennessee and saw where ground met sky in Oklahoma and in Texas. I saw God in a monumental way. When we arrived in Wheeler, Texas, I was surprised to see such a small place. The town was built on a square. One red light served the whole town, and stores were on a square around a huge courthouse in the center. The history we realized was amazing and the cowboy theme hung heavy. Cowboys walked down sidewalks jingling from spurs on the backs of their boots. If I hadn't known better, I would have thought that we had just driven into a western theme park. In just a couple of days, Junior landed a job at one of the three gas stations pending a haircut. No hippie-looking people in this town! So I used my haircutting skills, and he went right back and got the job. He would be pumping gas and washing windshields, fixing flats and brakes. He enjoyed that job and worked there for a few years. Meantime, I got the kids ready to start school. We found a rent house in a neighboring town called Mobeetie, twelve miles away. This town had an interesting history and is smaller than wheeler. The school was smaller, and this is where the kids went to school. It was a one building school that taught grades K–12. There were four kids in the first grade. The other grades averaged similar. The history of this town is online and is so amazing. I fell in love with history while in Texas. I wish I could have fallen in love with my husband as fast, but that didn't happen for either of us for a few years. It did happen eventually and has lasted as of this writing, forty years. We love each other dearly. A lady we met in Mobeetie was ninety years old. She told us about how she remembered as a young child walking behind a wagon headed to Texas.

She said that they had to walk most of the way because the oxen had to last the whole trip and needed to pull less weight. Her story telling was as interesting as she was. She still dressed like the 1800s. She had on a prairie hat, long to her feet dress, and wore boot shoes that she had to close with a hook.

She inspired me to study the history of Mobeetie, and then I began to study the Bible better. I learned to be curious, and once I got a clue, I kept digging to get the answers. I never did well in school, and then at twenty-eight years old, it seemed that my mind had been opened to learning. It was in being inspired to research it and know how to study. Some time passed and we moved to another house. The house was really awesome. The one neighbor was two miles away. They were across the street from us but their driveway was two miles long. There was another house right on our road going back to the main highway about five miles from us. The house we rented had a living room and a dining room on the front of the house.

Once you went through the door from the living room, you entered the little rectangular hall. From that hall were two bedrooms straight across from the living room door. Standing at the living room door facing the bedrooms were a kitchen to the left and a bathroom to the right. Right in the middle of the hall, the attic ladder was down and stayed down as there was a bedroom up there and Junior and I took that one. A few months later, Michael had a cold with a slight fever and the school had me pick him up. So I stayed home with him instead of going back to work. We had a big satellite dish. This was the eighties, so this dish was sixteen feet across. It was a huge mesh disc with a remote inside to turn it to gain channels. We received channels from all over the world. It was really awesome. On the remote were twenty-four positions and twenty-four channels in each position. There were a lot of repeats. Ahh, those were the days of free cable/satellite TV. Michael had it on a lower position and was watching Disney. I went to the kitchen to make us some chicken soup. Michael came into the kitchen to tell me something as I got our TV tables and we took our food to the living room. I had already turned the stove off and turned off the light on my way out of the kitchen. When we reached the living room, Michael was saying, "Hey, the dish changed positions and channel number." He busied himself with correcting it as I sat preparing to eat and didn't think about the satellite dish changing all by itself.

As Michael was returning to sit, he noticed the kitchen light on and asked in a correcting the adult way, if he should turn it off. Turning my head to one side, I searched my memory for the action of turning the light off. I was sure I had. When Michael entered the kitchen, he exclaimed, "Hey, Mom, the stove is on!" I jumped up and saw all four burners on high! Now, I knew for certain that I had turned the stove off, and I had only used one burner! I turned them off and Michael flipped the light switch. Back at our tables, we picked up our spoons, and we heard the toilet flush. The bathroom was just on the other side of the living room wall behind Michael. We looked at each other with wide eyes and jumped up. As we entered the bathroom, we got there just in time to see the water leaving the bowl. We laughed and joked, saying things like, "We must have ghost that lived before the inside flushing toilet and electricity." We loved living in the house. It was so private with no neighbors to speak of and a lot of acreage that was all around us leased out for pasture land.

The kids and I would go on long hikes across the pasture land and down to what we called an oasis. There was a good-sized creek that split around a small island and a large grove of plum bushes that supplied us with jam and fruit snacks. One day, the rancher that leased the pasture land saw us walking back toward the house, and after talking a bit with him, he looked at us from his horse and asked where our guns were. "We didn't have any," we replied, and he warned us not to walk the "prairie" without one due to badgers, rattlesnakes, and wildcats. Yikes! Well, we didn't have any guns, and I didn't know how to use one. So we walked on the road a bit, but it was no fun. Someone told us that walking on the long white clay road wasn't any different from the prairie because the wild animals didn't know the difference. We missed our oasis, though. Life was good there. Junior wanted to refinish the hard wood floors so we got busy on that project and life went on, normal…for a while.

One night, while asleep (in the attic bedroom), I awoke to a weird sensation. I was almost standing on my head. I woke to see the foot of the bed raised high in the air. I was so stunned and couldn't make a sound at first. Then I tried to wake Junior (my husband), but he was deep in sleep. I was about to yell when the bed dropped to the floor. The slats came out and the mattress went off the rails and rested on the floor as well. I tried again to wake him, but all of a sudden, I felt myself falling to sleep. I was reminded of what had happened the next morning when I saw the evidence. I tried to tell Junior about it but he didn't believe me and made a joke of it. I was amazed at how he slept through it, and I just fell back to a hard sleep.

A few days later, Junior and I got up before dawn, as usual, to get him off to work. It was still dark when he left, and the kids were still asleep. The attic had a typical attic ladder and stayed down all the time. It had thin handrails made of a rope on either side. The only light on was the one in the kitchen and a lamp in the attic bedroom. I went to go upstairs to get dressed before waking the kids. Rounding the ladder and then grabbed the handrails and this put me facing the kitchen and the bathroom to my back. On the right side of the kitchen door was a long mirror. As I took one step up on the ladder, I saw in the mirror behind me, which would be in the bathroom doorway, a pair of legs. White legs, with a good deal of hair on them, looked like a young man's legs from the thighs down as the rest was in the shadow of the bathroom. Immediately I thought it was my sixteen-year-old son, Tommy. So I turned around to say "Boo!" and "Good morning," but no one was there. I turned on the light, and no one! Right away, I checked Tommy's room and he was sound asleep. Before the kids left for school, I told them about it and that we would be anointing the house when they got home. We did just that and as we anointed each wall, we commanded that all unclean spirits had to leave and not return as long as we lived there. They left and we were not bothered again.

"Heal the sick, cleanse the lepers, and raise the dead, cast out devils. Freely ye have received, freely give" (Matt. 10:8).

Right after we arrived in Texas, I had to have surgery. After having delivered my daughter Brandy five years earlier, I had heavy bleeding. Two D&C procedures had helped each time, but the problem would reoccur. My new husband and I could not consummate our new marriage until I found what was causing the continuing problem. I compiled a list of gynecologist and prayed for the Lord to help me to choose the right doctor. I chose Dr. Price. He was in Pampa, the closest city that was larger than Mobeetie, and I had a good feeling about him. Dr. Price was somewhere in his early forties maybe, and he seemed pretty knowledgeable. He would remove my tubes, and since I would no longer need my uterus, that would come out as well. I looked forward to the surgery. It came and went with no issue. Just after the surgery, Dr. Price came to a groggy me and said, "It went well," and that he had taken my appendix while he was in there. I recovered, the marriage to my husband began, and all was good.

I went to work cleaning motel rooms in another small town. A few years later, I started to swell all over. My hands and feet started first, then my face, before I knew it, I was swollen all over. Junior was working in the oil field. On an oil rig, they had real long shifts and if the relieving crew couldn't make it for whatever reason, then he'd have to stay on until the shift after that. I couldn't walk, and I depended on him to take me to the bathroom, to bed, and to make the kids dinner. Lucky for me, that they were not little babies and could at least make a sandwich and cook simple dishes. I knew that I had Candida, a yeast infection. Usually confined, it can spread over the entire body. So we went to Pampa to see Dr. Price without an appointment as he would take a walk in. When we walked in the office, it was empty with the exception of two office personnel. They told us that he had left his wife and kids and ran off to Florida with his office manager. We were stunned, and now I would have to find another doctor. There was a clinic at the Amarillo hospital on the other side of Pampa that we decided to go to because we just didn't have any money. After going there, we were told to go to see Dr. Hands. Dr. Hands agreed to see me for a very low fee. He told me that I had cyst coating each of my ovaries, and he recommended hormone therapy for three months. I took the hormones but saw little change.

The treatment works on the premise that it would shut down the ovaries and give them a change to heal on their own. When I went back to him, I had the agreement of the Texas rehabilitation for payment for the surgery that he now wanted to do. Dr. Hands would be retiring at the end of that year, and I was the last new patient that he would ever see. He wanted to go in and scrape my ovaries, like barnacles on a ship, to remove the cyst. After the surgery, Dr. Hands came to my bedside and to a groggy me and said, "I thought you said you had your tubes removed?" I nodded yes. He said, "No, ma'am, they were still there. They had been burned in several places that looked like for sterilization, and they had been infected for so long that they were rotting. They were causing the ovaries to rot too. Unfortunately, I wasn't able to save the ovaries." I was put on hormone pills until I turned forty-two when they were then decreased.

I was upset with God for many years because I thought he had led me to Dr. Price whom I blamed for causing me a lifelong problem. After the second surgery, I was sitting up in bed at home, was startled, which caused my body to jerk backward. When I did, I felt like a rubber band had snapped inside where my left ovary used to be. My entire left leg and across my pelvic went numb and pain went halfway down my right leg. Junior took me back to see Dr. Hands, but he didn't know what had happened and told me that he couldn't say if it would get better. He said it could have been a nerve or a tendon; he just didn't know. I was being pushed in a wheel chair and was in a lot of pain. He told me to take Tylenol, and it didn't help. He recommended compression hose. Junior would have to put them on me, and they would feel so very good and the pain would subside for about one minute and before he could get the second one all the way to my thigh the pain would be back. I'd scream in pain and cry out.

Poor man took them off and put them on me over and over just for a few moments of relief. Being in this condition, we felt the best thing to do was to go back to North Carolina. We sold all we had and headed east. We had been in Texas for nine years. It took more than a year for me to rehab myself from the wheelchair and then the walker. Finally I would walk again. I tried not to have bitterness toward God. Years later, when I was praying, I asked the Lord why he had let the first doctors burn my tubes and then why did he lead me to Dr. Price. He answered me simply, "I had to keep you from dying of ovarian cancer." I fell to the floor in a weeping heap. All I went through was to save my life. I learned that God works through the powers and availabilities of this natural realm, and we must thank him for all things good and even for what we "*think*" is bad.

The year 1993 was a very spiritually busy year for our family. Not on our accord, but the Spirit was really moving. The Spirit revealed many things, and many that came to our meetings had received the Holy Ghost. My niece Angie had come to visit that summer for a month. She is my brother's child, and I had not gotten to see her very often, so this would be a getting acquainted visit. It didn't take very long before she was comfortable with all of us and us with her.

She was twelve and inquisitive about the Lord. Angie sat in on our prayer meetings and was very quiet; before we knew it, she was yelling for Jesus and receiving the Holy Ghost. She was desperate to get baptized then. It was midweek, and she was insisting on getting baptized immediately. I asked if she could wait until the weekend as the only ones around that day was Michael, my son, and I. All the rest were out working. She was adamant about going then, so Michael and I took her to Lake Norman. When we got there, we were disappointed to see that a couple had taken our favorite spot. They had a blanket spread out for what looked like a picnic. We liked that section because there was part of a paved road that was partially in the water. A lot of rural land had been flooded to make the lake. It was also a more private place. So we walked on past that nice section and headed to a marshy section just past the picnickers. I asked Michael to perform the baptism since he had recently been ordained by the Lord, and I really didn't want to sink up to shins in the silt. They made their way slowly in the water and moved along the bank. I thought maybe they were looking for a better bottom. The walking was stirring up the silt, and it began to make the water look a bit murky. He baptized her in the name of Jesus, and she then started to wring out her long blond hair.

Michael came out of the water, and I handed him a towel. As he got the towel, Angie yelled up to the top of the bank, "Aunt Beth, what is that?" I couldn't see from the top of the bank to where she was pointing. I called back to her that it was probably turtleheads. We had seen turtles sticking their heads up out of the water many times. She was very sure that it was not turtles. I asked Michael to go back in the water so that he could look from her angle. When he was positioned beside of her, she pointed and he squinted. "Mom," he said with a slight urgency, "you need to come and see this and hurry." I quickly kicked off my shoes and winced when I hit the muddy silt. It squished between my toes all the way to where they stood. Michael pointed, and I saw nothing, I guess because I was still looking for something that looked like turtleheads. Then Michael asked if I saw the ripples in the water. I looked and saw some small ripples (tiny waves) coming toward us. He said, "Now look to the center of it." I furrowed my brow and he said looks like someone threw a rock in the water and the ripples are moving away from the center. "Yeah, I see it now." He instructed me further by saying, "Now in the center look just above the water."

There in the center of the ripples were demons flowing up out of the water. There were so many that you could hardly tell where one ended and another started. They went up like a water fountain, and then they would fall gently to just above the water and while hovering there they moved off in every direction except toward us. "What is it?" Angie asked again.

"It's demons that came out of you," I told her and she gasped as we watched them floating above the water.

"It's all those lies," she whispered. They suddenly turned to head to where the couple had been picnicking. We watched until they went behind the tree line and gauged when they would reach the couple. Just as we knew they had reached them, we heard the couple yelling and cussing at each other. The man yelled at her that they would just get the blank out of there. Michael looked at us and said, "I think we should go too." We did just that, and to this day, that was the most eventful baptism we have ever had.

One night in a prayer meeting at Michael's house, 7:00 p.m. rolled around, and we had been in Bible study and prayer since early afternoon. People would come and go during our service as they could go on for days. We were sitting on the floor and everyone was praying in the spirit.

"But the hour cometh and now is when the TRUE worshippers shall worship in spirit and in truth: for the Father seeketh such to worship him" (John 4:23 KJV).

We didn't pray silently. A few of us would get quite loud as the spirit reached a crescendo. Because so many left and returned or left and someone different came in. I didn't pay any attention to that noise. The one coming in would just chime in to the prayer. We didn't pray for specifics only praising and thanking the father. Praying in tongues is us allowing the spirit to speak to Jesus on our behalf. Jesus, in turn, makes the plea to the father on our behalf. Without allowing the tongues the spirit cannot make intercession for us.

> Likewise the Spirit also helpeth our infirmities: for we know not what we should pray for as we ought: but the Spirit itself maketh intercession for us with groanings which cannot be uttered.
>
> And he that searcheth the hearts knoweth what [is] the mind of the Spirit, because he maketh intercession for the saints according to [the will of] God. (Romans 8:26–27 KJV)

So when the door opened and closed, I didn't think much of it and didn't pause. Only a couple of people greeted the new arrivals. I then heard my daughter Brandy's voice and my nephew Eugene was with her. Eugene had been living in Arkansas and had an on again/ off again relationship with the Lord, which is really no relationship at all. Jesus wants 100 percent. I had not heard from or seen Eugene in some time and didn't know where he stood with the Lord.

As soon as they were seated on the floor, and everyone had resumed their focus on Jesus, the spirit spoke through me, saying to Eugene, "So, Gene, I see you are in my face, for how long this time?"

He and Brandy laughed a little, and when the praying stopped for a break, they explained that when Brandy had picked him up, he had told her that he was going to get in Jesus's face and stay there.

"For if ye turn again unto the Lord, your brethren and your children shall find compassion before them that lead them captive, so that they shall come again into this land: for the Lord your God is gracious and merciful, and will not turn away his face from you, if ye return unto him" (2 Chron. 30:9 KJV).

Maranda and I went to Walmart in about '98. She had to pick up a few things, and I was just browsing. She was focused on her list, and I lingered on aisles checking out new lines of different products. I love window shopping sometimes because you really take the time to see so many items that ordinarily are overlooked as Maranda was doing then. She would check off an item and then head for the next item, knowing exactly what item she wanted. She needed ink pens. As she zeroed in on her kind, I looked them all over. I saw a package that had all foreign words on it. "Hey," I said. "This is all in a foreign language." She had her back to me and, with a nonchalant reply, said, "Well, we know that one wasn't made here." I shrugged and agreed, hanging the package back up.

As we were finished with the shopping, and she was checking out, I went to the magazine rack across from the registers and without touching them I read their titles and the writing on the covers. I glanced over at another rack with some nibbles and then back to the magazines. All the magazines were in a foreign language that I didn't know, but some of the letters looked English but were backward.

Mouth open in surprise, I turned to yell for Maranda, but she was several registers away. Besides, she was in the middle of the transaction at the checkout. I turned back to the magazines to look at them again, but now they were all normal.

> But blessed are your eyes, for they see, and
> your ears, for they hear. (Matt. 13:16 KJV)

> They say unto him: Lord, that our eyes may
> be opened. (Matt. 20:33 KJV)

Cabarrus County, in the city of Concord, North Carlina, was having a free mammogram week. I had not had one in forever, so I decided to go for it. Days afterward, I got a call telling me that I needed to have a second mammogram as they saw a mass in my left breast. They were sending me to a radiologist in Charlotte, North Carolina. It was scheduled for the following Monday. Each weekend I went to stay at my mother's. That weekend it was me, Mother and my eighteen-year-old daughter. We had a good long praying session that included laying hands on me about the mass.

> Is any sick among you? Let him call for the
> elders of the church, and let them pray over him,
> anointing him with oil in the name of the Lord.
> And the prayer of faith shall save the sick,
> and the Lord shall raise him up; and if he has
> committed sins, they will be forgiven him. (James
> 5:14–15 KJV)

I slept on the living room sofa that night, which was unusual as I usually slept in mother's room on the cot where we would talk and giggle half the night. I wanted to lay there thank God for my life in him and praise him for the healing that I knew would come. Also I was so very tired and I wanted to drift off and get some rest. In mother's room we would have been talking all night. I generally like a dark room and the street light filtering through the blinds and curtains didn't even bother me. The light was very dim, and it took some time before my eyes adjusted to the semidark room. Sometime through the night, I was awakened by pressure on my chest. At first, I thought that I was being attacked by a man because all I saw was this darker than the room shadow moving off of me and going to the floor. I was gasping for breath and was frozen to the sofa. I sat up then and saw the "thing." It looked like the shape of a maggot and was moving like a maggot would. It was the size of a large exercise ball. It wiggled until it went right through the wall leading outside. It was a demon! Demons can take any shape and can enter any living thing.

"Submit yourselves therefore to God. Resist the devil and he will flee from you" (James 4:7 KJV).

On Monday, I went with confidence and without fear to the radiologist. I received a mammogram and the radiologist said it looked like a starburst was coming out of my left breast. They decided to do a sonogram, and praise God, there was nothing to be seen. It was still showing a starburst the last one I had done. They are puzzled, but I just smile, knowing that I was healed of the demonic mass.

In 2012, I was on I-85 on a hot day in June. I had an hour's drive so I called Junior to chat. No sooner than we had started to talk, I noticed in the clear blue sky something dark and moving. It looked like a crocodile. It appeared to be flying, yet it had no wings. Dragon kept coming to my mind. It was like a charcoal drawing but in a light gray. I noticed that it wasn't ghost like as I could not see through it. It was solid. The upper part rolled in the sky. It was after a mouse, a mouse that was running on his hind legs. He wore a burnt orange vest and shorts. He wore no shoes but wore a black French artist cap. The "dragon" rolled and twisted as the mouse ran with a look of fear on his face.

Suddenly trees obstructed my view, and as I drove, I continued to describe it to him. I was anxious to see that part of the sky again. When I finally rounded a curve and could see the sky, the images had moved. They had not disappeared as I had feared it might, but the scene had changed. The images weren't moving now but looked as a still. The body of the crock (dragon) had turned its body almost into a "U" shape. The mouse's body had been bitten completely in two. A stunned expression was on the mouse's face with his head and torso to the right part of the sky and his bottom half to the left. In cartoons, there would be lines drawn to show that a fire cracker had exploded and these same lines were between the mouse's body parts. "Oh no," I said to Junior and described the scene to him. Then the images began to blow away as wind would slowly scatter sand.

In the weeks that followed, I prayed daily. I'd walk around the backyard, asking God to tell me the meaning of this vision. One day, as I prayed and praised, and again asked for the meaning, he spoke to me, saying, "Revelation 13:7."

"And it was given unto him to make war with the saints and to overcome them. And power was given him over all kindred's and tongues, and nations" (Rev. 13:7 KJV).

So I read it and found this in Daniel: "And he shall speak great words against the most high and shall wear out the saints of the most high and think to change times and laws and they shall be given into his hand until a time and times and the dividing of time" (Dan. 7:25 KJV).

The "he" here is the antichrist. Time, times, and half a time is three and a half years.

Receiving the Holy Ghost is the ultimate goal after first believing in Jesus because the Bible reads, "But ye are not in the flesh, but in the Spirit, *if* so be that the Spirit of God dwell *in you*. Now if any man has not the Spirit of Christ, *he is none of his*" (Rom. 8:9 KJV).

The Holy Ghost is the third part of the Godhead. He is symbolized in the Bible by a dove, a flame, wind, a cloud, water, oil, a seal, a hand, a finger, and is the breath of God. He is all-knowing, omnipotent. The Holy Ghost has a mind and a will. He has feelings, he teaches, he intercedes, he speaks, he testifies. He can be grieved, lied to, and he can be blasphemed, which is the *unforgivable sin*. He is a part of the trinity. The Holy Ghost is always behind Jesus. How does one blaspheme the Holy Ghost? By criticizing his work or him, or contributing to Satan the work of the Holy Ghost. Many make fun of speaking in tongues or the wild movements someone may make while being moved by the Holy Ghost and/or contribute it to the devil. Be very careful what you say, attributing to Satan what is of God is the *unforgiveable* sin. He is the executor (carry out the will) of God. The Holy Ghost is the one who calls you and woos you to come to Jesus. Let's explain it with electricity. The wiring is in the wall and is not seen. This could be a representation of God. The light bulb and the light are indicative of Jesus. It is what can be seen. If we got close to the bulb, we would feel the heat of it and that is the presence of the Holy Ghost. He is also the unseen power, the electricity. We are the light switch; we have to agree to see the light. Another analogy of the Godhead is this: looking at an egg we see the shell; this represents Jesus. He can be seen and must be broken for you to reach God. The yoke represents God. It is the major treasure of the egg. It has the power to create life. Then there is the white, once the egg is broken, it is released and flows and goes where it will, just as the Holy Ghost goes about flowing where he will.

The Holy Ghost is a person. You can only blaspheme a person. The Holy Ghost teaches. He speaks when he arrives in you to testify of Jesus (speaking in tongues, heavenly language).

"But when the Comforter is come, whom I will send unto you from the father, even the spirit of truth, which proceedeth from the Father, he shall testify of me" (John 15:26).

No one can say that Jesus is Lord except by the Holy Ghost. In other words, if you don't have the baptism of the Holy Ghost, he is not your Lord.

The Holy Ghost seals you. He will lead you gently or drive you. He heals. He will speak through you in divers (different known languages) and in the tongues of angels or speak through you in your own language to someone else (whatever their language is). Say you are witnessing and words just pours out of you and even while you are speaking you are thinking, Wow this is good stuff. This is the Holy Ghost speaking through you to the other person. Ananias and his wife were punished by death because they lied, not to God or the apostles, but to the Holy Ghost! The Holy Ghost is a gift and that doesn't mean that you don't ask for him, no, you don't just wait around for him to decide to gift you with himself. You go to Jesus for the Holy Ghost to enter into you because he is a gift, means that you can't do anything as in works to attain him and you can't buy him. Being a gift doesn't mean that he is optional because he is the third part of the salvation process and is necessary. Jesus was saying in John 3:5–8 (KJV), "The wind bloweth where it listeth, and thou hearest the sound thereof, but canst not tell whence it cometh, and whither it goeth: so is every one that is born of the Spirit."

"The wind is the spirit. He goes where he will. You hear the wind rustle leaves and the trees sway as it moves, the wind will make whistling or howling sounds as it becomes present. The spirit is the same."

You don't see him but you hear him when he becomes present. When he enters into a person, he will make sounds through them. So is every person who is born into the kingdom.

In Acts 2, we see what happened when the wind entered the upper room and the disciples received the Holy Ghost:

> And when the day of Pentecost was fully come, they were all with one accord in one place.
>
> And suddenly there came a sound from heaven as of a rushing mighty wind, and it filled all the house where they were sitting.
>
> And there appeared unto them cloven tongues like as of fire, and it sat upon each of them.
>
> And they were all filled with the Holy Ghost, and began to speak with other tongues, as the Spirit gave them utterance. (Acts 2:1–4 KJV)

Let me say it in my own words: And when it was the height of the Pentecost celebration, they (disciples) were all together in the same place.

Suddenly a sound, a spiritual sound like a mighty wind filled the whole house and what looked like a flame that was split in two was on each one's head.

They were then filled with the Holy Ghost and they each began speaking in tongues as the spirit caused them to speak (utter). The split flame was the shape of the Hebrew letter "shin." This is the first letter in the word Shaddai, which means "God." There is a blessing that the high priest would give and he would hold his hands as Spock did in Star Trek because that is where he copied it from…his Jewish priest. So when this experience happened to them, they knew immediately that it was from God.

So why weren't they born again before the day of Pentecost? (Read John 7:39.) They were walking with Jesus, and they themselves had to of been baptized by John the Baptist as two of them had started out as John's disciples. Jesus had the disciples baptizing right down the river from where John was baptizing. So weren't the disciples saved? The answer is no. They didn't even change until after they received the Holy Ghost. Some people think that they received the Holy Ghost when Jesus breathed on them.

Here is that scripture:

> And when he had so said, he shewed unto them his hands and his side. Then were the disciples glad, when they saw the Lord.
>
> Then said Jesus to them again, Peace be unto you: as my Father hath sent me, even so send I you.
>
> And when he had said this, he breathed on them, and saith unto them, Receive ye the Holy Ghost:
>
> Whosoever sins ye remit, they are remitted unto them; and whosoever sins ye retain, they are retained. (John 2:20–23 KJV)

We see from the scripture that this happened after Jesus had risen from the dead. He had shown them his hands and his pierced side. Then in verse 22, he breathed on them. Remember how God breathed life into Adam. Jesus sent life to the disciples. I know that they didn't receive the Holy Ghost inside of them because of these next verses.

> And I will pray the Father, and he shall give
> you another Comforter, that he may abide with
> you forever;
>
> Even the Spirit of truth; whom the world
> cannot receive, because it seeth him not, neither
> knoweth him: but ye know him; for he dwelleth
> with you, and shall be in you. (John 14:16, 17
> KJV)

The Holy Ghost lived (abided, dwelled) *with them* but was not *in* them. When Jesus breathed on them, the spirit would now get them ready for receiving. When you cry out to God for deliverance, the Holy Ghost comes to walk "with" you, the Christian world calls this saved and sadly most people stop here thinking this is good, and there isn't anything more to attain. When the Holy Ghost has readied you, *and you seek him,* he will enter into you. Different people have different experiences receiving the Holy Ghost. I said "Jesus" over and over faster and faster. No one told me to do it that way, I just did. It worked. I was crying and practically screaming his name. I began to speak in tongues. It was when I could not control my speech that the Holy Ghost took control.

So I sounded like this: "Jesus, Jesus, Jesus, Geeda, Geeda, Geegeegeegeegee," and then I sounded like you do when your teeth are chattering from the cold and a hum can't help but develop. After receiving him, the Holy Ghost will drive you to go where you need to go. He will use your mouth to speak, teach, and preach. He will make gentle suggestions and many times sends to you strong urges to follow his lead. Remember Romans 8:9 that tells you that if you do not have the Holy Ghost in you then you do not belong to the kingdom of God.

I implore you to continue to seek for the baptism of the Holy Ghost after your believing in Jesus. Remember in Acts 19, Paul asked some of John's disciples if they had received the Holy Ghost since they had become believers and they had not. Paul baptized them in the name of Jesus, laid hands on them, and they received the infilling of the Holy Ghost, spoke in tongues, and prophesied. Search the scriptures for yourself to find out when is a person "born again."

If you think you are born again, check with the scriptures in Acts to see if you really are because church leaders were deceived and for more than a thousand years have been passing the deception on to you. It's the blind leading the blind. Read the scriptures for yourself. The scriptures say to believe in Jesus not receive him or accept him into your heart but to believe in him. In Acts 2, Peter says to repent, be baptized in water (in Jesus's name) and then to receive the Holy Ghost. The apostate church will have you believe that you repent and accept Jesus in your heart and automatically receive the gift of the Holy Ghost as you are baptized in the name of the father, son, and Holy Ghost. I don't want you to be deceived and miss going to heaven. Just read it with study and intent to see the truth that is hidden in plain sight. Peter opened the three doors to the kingdom. The first door in Acts 2 was to bring in the Jews (to the Jew first), three thousand believed in Jesus and received the Holy Ghost. In Acts 2, the now apostles (after receiving the Holy Ghost) were speaking in the unknown tongue not in different languages and they were falling about as the crowd thought they were drunk. In Acts 8, Phillip was preaching to the Samaritans. Many had believed and were baptized in (Jesus's name) but none had received the Holy Ghost. What? They believed and we know that the apostles and Phillip would have taught repentance. Phillip was a spirit-filled evangelist under the apostles' teaching. None had received the Holy Ghost, even though they had gone the route of most church doctrines.

The apostles sent Peter because he had the keys. So read what happened when Peter got there. He laid hands on them, and they received the Holy Ghost. It doesn't say that the Samaritans spoke in tongues because Luke was more interested in showing Simons not so right heart. However, how did they know that none had gotten the Holy Ghost before Peter arrived and how did they know that they received after Peter and John laid hands on them? In Acts 10, Peter opened the door for the Gentiles to believe and receive, and we can see that they received as Peter was still talking. In verses 44–48, it describes how they received and how they all knew that they were filled with the Holy Ghost *because* they all (Peter and the Jews with him) heard them speaking in tongues. And then after they received, they were baptized (in Jesus's name) not in Father, son, and Holy Ghost. The spirit didn't come into them when they were baptized in water, not in any of the three nations.

I've just given you highlights of my life in Christ; I hope it got you interested in seeking truth for yourself. The apostles were with Jesus the Christ for three years, and he told them things that he told no other. Please don't accept any body's word about *your* salvation. No one will be blamed for your choices, but you. I had to study it myself because I do not want to hear, "Depart from me, for I know you not."

FRANCES

I enjoyed going out to bars, dancing, and making friends. I thought I was a good person. There was no way that I would ever hurt anyone. One day, I lost interest in going to bars for dancing and the friends I thought I had pulled away from me. I wanted to be around my family. My daughter Beth lived for Jesus, and I lived next door to her. I saw her with her children, and she made a game with them. She would march around the coffee table singing, and they would follow behind her singing "When the Saints Go Marching In," even the poodle dog followed.

After a few times around the table, they knelt down on their knees and prayed. Even the dog put his paws on the table and put his head on his paws. I couldn't believe this family. How beautiful they were in the Lord. Every day this went on. Beth prayed all day in whatever she did, and she made her life beautiful in Jesus. I asked her a lot of questions, and she answered me explaining things where I could understand. One day I went to Beth's next door. I waited at the door as she was sweeping up right in front of the door. As I waited, I looked up into the sky and I saw a huge stand like a preacher would stand behind to preach. There was a very thick book on it, and the pages were turning. I told Beth what I was seeing. By the time she had the baby moved and the door opened, the vision had gone. She was disappointed because she had wanted to see it too. She told me it was the book of life, and God was turning the pages, looking for my name. I said, "Why would my name not be there? I love Jesus."

She said, "But, Mother, you don't have the Holy Ghost." I was afraid then. "I don't?" I asked and she said, "Mother, you have to receive the spirit of Jesus In you."

"Well, how would I do that?" Because if I didn't have him, I wanted him. I wanted my name in the book. We were in the kitchen then and she had finished washing dishes. She said, "All you have to do is to get on your knees and lift your hands and praise him."

"Would you show me how?" I didn't want to do it wrong so she started telling me how again and I said, "No, show me how," so she got on her knees and lifted her hands, and she said, "I praise you, Jesus. Jesus, Jesus." I stopped her then and told her to get up and right in front of the kitchen sink, where she had knelt, I knelt. I lifted my hands, and I said to Jesus that I praised him and I said for him to take me and love me. I said a lot of other stuff, but I found out later that I only needed to say his name.

I was crying and I was trembling inside so much that I felt it on the outside. Beth had been standing behind me up against the kitchen sink. Suddenly I felt her dump some water on my head. I felt the spirit then moving in me. I got up and was still shaking. My mouth quivered but no sound came out. Beth was so thrilled but she was concerned that I had not spoken in a heavenly language. I couldn't help that it didn't happen but I trusted her that it should have. She told me to keep praising him just like I did that day and it would come. So it was that Henry and I got married and we moved to Macon, North Carolina, to live on his cabin cruiser.

Only a few weeks had passed since I received the Holy Ghost. The lake was beautiful, and I enjoyed being there. My new husband was gone a lot, and while I was alone, I read the Bible and prayed. I kept myself busy with checking the homes around the lake to make sure they were okay. I was busy all the time. I like to be active. I walked through the woods with my yellow lab dog. I began to have visions. I started to see the spirit realm. I saw angels from time to time. Beth came to see me, and we prayed together. We walked through the woods together and Beth baptized me in the lake. It was an awesome day. I felt so new that day and after that I began to speak in tongues. What a wonderful day. I am so glad to live this life.

> But ye, beloved, building up yourselves on
> your most holy faith, praying in the Holy Ghost.
> (Jude 1:20 KJV)

> And they were all filled with the Holy
> Ghost, and began to speak with other tongues,
> as the Spirit gave them utterance. (Acts 2:4 KJV)

> But ye are not in the flesh, but in the Spirit,
> *if* so be that the Spirit of God dwell in you. Now
> if any man has not the Spirit of Christ, he is none
> of his. (Rom. 8:9 KJV)

I went with four of my grandkids for a walk. We went about five miles in the country, and about one-fourth miles from our house we saw a side road and decided to take it. It was a circle road with just a few homes on it. On several phone poles, there was a picture of a mean looking guard dog. This was done several times before we got to the house. I told the children that there could be no dog in the world that could look like that picture because he looked so mean. As we were walking past the driveway on the street in front of this house, here comes the guard dog! I could not believe how he came charging for us! Just as he got to me and the children I called out "Jesus, Jesus!" He then looked over our heads and growled and started backing up. His eyes were on and off of us. He turned around and started back to the house. The owner came running out to the yard. He saw the dog going back to the house. He just stood and scratched his head. He was shocked because we were not hurt. Jesus stopped the dog from hurting us. As we walked on one of the boys got stung by a Bee. I laid my hand on the place that was swelling. Right away it started going down.

"Confess your faults one to another, and pray one for another, that ye may be healed. The effectual fervent prayer of a righteous man availeth much" (James 5:16 KJV).

Then we laughed and talked and played on the road at the end of our walk. Before starting back, we decided to go on across to the end of another road. When we get to the end of it, my granddaughter, the oldest of them, said "I have never seen a vision in the air." Just as she looked up, she saw a word written so plain: SOON.

The sky was blue, and there were no white clouds in the air—only the word. We were so happy that God loved us that much! Then we turned around to start back to our house. Suddenly my granddaughter said, "Look!" We followed her gaze. There was a lady in a white dress. She was so beautiful. I told the children, "Now you cannot say that you have never seen a vision."

I've seen a lot of visions through the years, and when Jesus told us to write them down, I almost didn't know where to start. Some of the visions are very long, and some are for only a few seconds. I'm going to share one of those short visions with you now. I saw this and then the Lord led me to the Bible verse later.

Most of my visions are seen in the sky, probably because I'm always looking up into the sky because I just see so much of God's glory there in the beauty of color, clouds, the sun, moon, and stars.

One day, as I was looking up at the clear blue sky, I saw a huge mouth. There was no face, just a mouth. The mouth was wide open and then hundreds and hundreds of people came gushing from it. I was puzzled for a while until I was led to read the following verse.

"So then because thou art lukewarm and am neither cold or hot, I will spew thee out of my mouth I didn't know what spew meant so I looked it up and it means" (Rev. 3:16 KJV).

Vomit: "To come forth in a flood or gush."

Some people receive the Holy Ghost, but they don't live for Jesus fully. They aren't living it by letting the world (sin and world ways) go. They read just enough Bible to keep them warm or they pray just enough so that there are prayers once in a while delivered to God. God wants your whole heart. You can't live like the devil and claim to have a life in Christ.

"Jesus said unto him, Thou shalt love the Lord thy God with all thy heart, and with all thy soul, and with all thy mind" (Matt. 22:37 KJV).

I love to live for the Lord. I love to pray and praise God when I cook or do housework. My husband was cruel toward me. He did not like my living for God. He did not understand my faith. So it had come to a separation. Jesus was trying to make me understand that it was okay to leave, yet I hesitated. I was standing in the living room looking out the window. My husband was sitting in his easy chair and I had a vision. I saw Jesus outside walking away from our place. Without thinking, I said out loud, "Don't leave me." Of course my husband thought I was talking to him, but he did not answer. Then I saw an angel in the huge jasmine vine that was running up the porch post. From inside the house, I could see and hear the bush shaking wildly. I got the message. I moved two hundred miles away. I am enjoying living for the Lord. My daughter is living with me now, and we have a prayer meeting in my house twice a week. Living for Jesus is a wonderful life.

My oldest daughter Maranda, her four children, and myself, moved into a very bad section of town. We didn't know it until a few nights later. We were very strong in spirit. We knew God would always take care of us, no matter where we lived. One night, I asked God to put a fence of angels around our place. I know God is very understanding. The next morning I sat on the side of the bed, and I looked out the window and was startled to see angels standing as a fence, side by side all in white. We didn't stay there long because we found another place. I know there was always an angel fence there surrounding us.

After I had married Henry, we went to live on his thirty-three-foot cabin cruiser. Oh, it was an old boat, but I thought it was so grand even with its faded paint and old upholstered table seats. I was so crazy about it. I fixed it up with new curtains that I made and covered the seat cushions with a pretty bright material. I talked Henry into cutting an opening in the floor of the bow so I could place butter and other items in plastic containers in the cold water that circulated through the bottom of the boat. I tied ropes onto the handle of gallon jugs of milk and juice and dropped them over the side of the boat into the water. Six packs of soda were done the same way. When Beth or Maranda came, there would be ice cold drinks. It was only about a month after we started living on the boat that I began to read the Bible. You see, I had received the Holy Ghost just before we got married and came to the boat. I was forty-two. Henry put out fish traps all around the lake, and I went around checking the traps everyday while Henry was at work. I read the Bible often, and after reading that, his hand is over the whole earth; I wondered, "How could God put his hand over the whole Earth?"

I stopped reading and walked out on the pier. The sun was so beautiful shining through the trees on the water, the trees beautiful with their different colored leaves. The sun danced over the water and sparkled like diamonds. As I looked up, I saw a man's arm from the elbow to the tip of the fingers. I was startled; I asked myself, *Why is there a hand in the air?* Over and over, I said this. I did not know what to think. I looked up again. The arm was long and strong-looking. As I looked across the water, I heard a voice in my head saying, "My hand is over the Earth." As I stood there looking across the water, I could see his hand over my head like the sky is over the Earth. Oh, what a sight that was! Only God could show this to me!

> Mine hand also hath laid the foundation of the earth, and my right hand hath spanned the heavens: when I call unto them, they stand up together. (Isa. 48:13 KJV)

Beth and I went to stay a week end with my other daughter, Maranda. We had a wonderful prayer time. Every one prayed for the skin tag above my upper lip to fall off. I forgot all about it. We went to bed, and I woke up with blood streaming from my lip. It was gone! I asked Beth, "What do I do?" I thought I was bleeding to death at first. She was half asleep and told me to put ice on it. I did so right away. It was bleeding so bad; I had hoped she knew what she was talking about. I was so new in Christ, and I was so afraid. I was just before saying that I wanted to go to the hospital when it stopped bleeding. I felt so ashamed then because I had doubted. After it was all over, I could see that faith is the key to God's healing. Believing that it would be removed, not being shocked that it was and having confidence that it would be okay would have been the key.

> Behold, his soul which is lifted up is not upright in him: but the just shall live by his faith. (Hab. 2:4 KJV)

> And this is the confidence that we have in
> him, that, if we ask any thing according to his
> will, he heareth us. (1 John 5:14 KJV)

One day just after I had started to speak in the unknown tongue, I was leaving the lake house when suddenly I got a glimpse of Jesus. I felt his arms around me. I was so happy of having been filled with the Holy Ghost. At this writing, it is twenty years filled with the spirit of Jesus.

"As for me, I will call upon God, and the Lord shall save me. Evening, and morning, and at noon, will I pray, and cry aloud; and he shall hear my voice" (Ps. 55:16, 17 KJV).

I was lying down for the night, thinking of Jesus and feeling so much love for him. I thought I saw something, so I turned onto my right side. I moved my head over on the pillow, and it moved too. I was curious, so I kept my head and my eyes very still. And then I saw it, a set of beautiful eyes looking at me. I saw much love in his eyes, and then I was so close that he was in my eyes, and I was in his eyes. What an experience that was! He was showing me that we are one.

> That they all may be one; as thou, Father,
> *art* in me, and I in thee, that they also may be
> one in us: that the world may believe that thou
> hast sent me.
>
> And the glory which thou gavest me I have
> given them; that they may be one, even as we
> are one: I in them, and thou in me, that they
> may be made perfect in one; and that the world
> may know that thou hast sent me, and hast loved
> them, as thou hast loved me.
>
> While I was living at the lake and Jesus was
> teaching me and showing me visions, I had read
> in the Bible about the Holy Land. I ask my Lord,
> show me the promise land, Jesus had said ask and
> ye shall see. (John 17:21, 22, 23 KJV)

So he gave me a glance of the promise land, its holy-looking and very green—just breathtaking. Thank you, Jesus.

> He maketh me to lie down in green pastures: he leadeth me beside the still waters. (Ps. 23:2 KJV)

> They drop upon the pastures of the wilderness: and the little hills rejoice on every side. (Ps. 65:12 KJV)

My grandson was five years old. One day he said to me "Grandmama, I have an angel in my eye."

I said, "What? You do?" So this went on a few days, and so one day I said to Jesus, "Let me see what is in Mike's eye." And there it was, in front of my right eye, not in it but about an inch in front of it. It was so hard to believe, but there it was. Visions from God are real. I don't know what that meant for him, but I know it was of God.

> It is not expedient for me doubtless to glory. I will come to visions and revelations of the Lord. (2 Cor. 12:1 KJV)

> For the promise is unto you, and to your children, and to all that are afar off, even as many as the Lord our God shall call. (Acts 2:39 KJV)

I love Jesus so much. I pray so often because I do love my Lord. The Bible teaches that if we are filled with the Holy Ghost that we need no man to teach us

> Let that therefore abide in you, which ye have heard from the beginning. If that which ye have heard from the beginning shall remain in you, ye also shall continue in the Son, and in the Father.

And this is the promise that he hath promised us, *even* eternal life.

These *things* have I written unto you concerning them that seduce you.

but the anointing which ye have received
of him abideth in you, and ye need not that
any man teach you: but as the same anointing
teacheth you of all things, and is truth, and is no
lie, and even as it hath taught you, ye shall abide
in him. (1 John 2:24–27 KJV)

So it happened that after I received the Holy Ghost and began
to speak in an unknown tongue, I would pray and then sing. He
began to show me signs and wonders. There was so much that I saw.
God has been good to me.

One day, I visited at my daughter Beth's house. Her husband's
friend was there. He was in his late twenties or early thirties. I wanted
so much to tell him about my good life, being so full of the spirit. I
wanted to talk to him and tell him how it happened, but he broke
in and started quoting scripture. I thought, *Great, he knows Jesus.*
He didn't use the word *Jesus, God, Lord, Christ,* or nothing like that.
So I thought no more about it until I went back to the boat where I
lived. The Lord showed me a vision. I saw lots of people falling, there
must have been hundreds and hundreds. It looked like a huge glass
that the people were falling behind. Then I saw a pair of hands on
the glass sliding down the glass. Then I saw his face. It was the young
man that I had met. He had horror on his face. Jesus let me know
that even though he could quote scripture, he did not know Jesus.
The Holy Bible says that if his spirit is not in you, that you do not
belong to him.

Think the way God thinks: "No man has ever seen, heard or
even imagined the wonderful things God has in store for those who
love the Lord" (1 Cor. 2:9 KJV).

No matter where in life you are right now, God has much more
in store for you. God wants to take you to new levels in every area of
your life. He wants to give you more wisdom, so you can make better

decisions. He wants to give you a stronger anointing so you can have greater influence. It wants to bless you financially so you can be a better blessing to others. Don't get stuck in the same old rut, there's so much more to life! God has new frontiers to explore and higher mountains to climb. I can tell you with confidence that your best days are out in front of you.

TOMMY

This is a testimony of my life with Jesus Christ. My mother had received the Holy Ghost before I was born. I'm the oldest of three. I have a brother, three years younger, and a sister, four years younger.

Our dad was hardly ever there, and when he was, I wished he weren't. He was an abusive husband to my mom. We lived with him for eight years. I didn't miss him when he was gone. I remember I was very young when my mother began to teach us about Jesus. Mom would get down on her knees in the living room and pray. Although I was very young and didn't understand what speaking in tongues was, I got down and prayed in my own words too.

I can remember mom having prayer meetings with two ladies that had introduced her to Jesus. They would sing and praise Jesus and have a good time in the spirit. Mom began working with a construction company and moved us to a small mobile home on a lake. It was a nice place as I remember it. We didn't have money, very many toys, or other things, but we were happy. We didn't have gas for the stove, so Mom made a grill out of cement blocks and a grate. We cooked everything outside. We would fish from our dock about every day, and we would have fish to eat. It was easy, simple, carefree living, to me anyway. I know, to Mom it wasn't as easy, but Jesus was still taking care of us and we would be all right.

I remember going to visit my grandmother. She had received the Holy Ghost soon after my mom had. She would tell us about the many visions that she had seen. I didn't know what a vision was, but I never questioned why she was able to see angels or Jesus in the sky. Grandma was very special in the fact that God taught her through visions. I believe that visions are very important, no matter how large or small. The Bible is full of tales about people seeing visions. I haven't had any visions yet, but I know I will. Prayer meetings have always been a big part of my life. We would have meetings with Grandma, my two aunts, and their kids, and we'd have a good ole time. I don't know how long those meetings would last, but I know it was usually late. We took turns meeting at each other's houses. Prayer would start with everyone forming a circle with everyone on their knees, and we'd just start praising Jesus. At that time, I didn't have the Holy Ghost so I just prayed by saying, "I praise you, Jesus." Mom, Grandma, and my two aunts had received and they would speak in tongues. Prayer meetings became more intense.

My brother and sister both received the Holy Ghost, as well as my cousins Eugene and his sister Janice. It took me longer, for some reason. I had demons that I couldn't let go of.

As the years went on, I started following what my friends were doing: drinking, cussing, viewing pornography, chewing tobacco, and etc. I slipped further from Jesus. Our families moved to different states, and our prayer meeting diminished to Mom and us three kids. I was approaching the young age of eighteen, and although I had quit drinking and was away from the porn, I still wasn't seeking Jesus. I started listening to more heavy metal music. I grew my hair long and pierced one ear. I began to dip snuff. Now that I think about it, I don't think I was away from the porn because I would clip pictures of half-naked women from regular magazines and hang them in my room. Even though I no longer drank alcohol, I started collecting beer memorabilia. My walls were plastered with beer logos. I had steins, clothes, and clocks. Anything with the Budweiser logo on it, I wanted. I still prayed with Mom, brother, and sister. I still wasn't seeking Jesus.

One night, while I was sleeping, I heard the sound of water sloshing. It was so loud that it woke me up. I looked down at the foot of my waterbed and saw that just one corner was shaking violently. Not the whole bed but just the mattress part, which was weird because I had a bed that was full motion and sent waves throughout with just a touch. At first, I thought that I was dreaming but knew that I was quite awake and frightened. The corner stopped shaking, but at that moment, a feeling started at my feet and slowly moved up my body. It was kind of like a chilled numbness. A paralysis was slowly moving up my body! I couldn't move my feet, knees, or legs, and then it went to my waist and into my chest where I could hardly breathe! My arms were outstretched, and the paralysis continued upward until I was paralyzed from the neck down. I tried to yell, but all that would come out was a tiny gasp. I was terrified! I tried screaming for Mom, but nothing would escape my mouth. I started saying Jesus's name over and over in my head, and I pleaded for him to help me.

Finally the paralysis started to go away, and I could say Jesus's name out loud. After it was completely gone, I yelled for Mom and then went to her room. After telling her what had happened, we prayed. I know it wasn't my imagination, and it wasn't a dream. I didn't go back to sleep that night.

Still I did not seek Jesus. *What was wrong with me?* I wondered. After graduating high school, I had taken a landscaping job. I still lived at home. I slipped even further from seeking Jesus. I was using horrible language, dipping like crazy, and going back into hard pornography. Mom would invite me to pray. I just made excuses not to go. Pornography was putting an even harder grip on me, and not only was I viewing magazines, but I was renting and buying movies. I knew it was wrong, but I couldn't stop. I wanted to but couldn't.

A couple of years passed, and I joined the National Guard. I went back to drinking a lot. I was getting worse. One day, I decided not to make an excuse not to go to prayer meeting. So I went. I had been feeling horribly guilty for the things that I had been doing. I needed to pray, so I took Mom up on her invitation. Besides myself was mom, my sister, brother, his wife and two kids. I started praying, asking Jesus for forgiveness, and I started crying. Jesus told me to picture a door and a key and then to put the key in the door and open it.

I did, and when I opened the door, I could feel the Holy Ghost filling me from the feet up. It was like someone had a pitcher of "tingle" and was pouring it in my head, and it was filling me from the feet up. It was an awesome feeling. I was crying and saying "I love you, Jesus" and then began speaking in tongues. My tongues to start off with sounded like a machine gun or a hard stutter. I began reading my Bible and praying more and more. I began to experience spiritual things. I was changing! As I grew in Jesus, my tongues changed also. I had changed and so it went, for a while. The world still had a stronghold on me because I still listened to heavy metal music, and I still went to heavy metal concerts. Then pornography demons came back stronger than ever before, and I gave into the temptation to buy magazines and movies. Even though I didn't want to, I did.

It wasn't long after that I proposed to my girlfriend in Texas and she moved to North Carolina to be with me. I got us a place to live, and we moved in together. It was rocky between us. I felt we were already married in the eyes of God, but I wasn't treating her like a wife. I was treating her like a roommate, which began to take its toll on our relationship. I wasn't living the life of Christ, the way I should have been. I know that had a lot to do with it. I was losing everything! I kept going to prayer meetings and that helped me a lot. I was still having problems living Jesus in front of Deana (my fiancée), so our relationship was not improving. Our prayer group started getting "messages" from the Lord about things to come. Things about how the Earth will go through changes. We also received personal messages and prophecies. The Lord had told me that Deana would leave me and that she would be pregnant when she left. This came true. She left me and went back to Texas. A month went by when she called to say that she had taken a test and was pregnant. In a way her leaving was a good thing because I realized how much I loved her.

I began to grow spiritually. I stopped dipping, cussing, viewing porn, etc. The spirit has moved me to jump around the room and shout. What a great feeling that is. One of the best feelings is to cry "in the spirit," to cry because you love Jesus and long to see his face.

My biological dad got in touch with me during that period. Naturally, I was apprehensive about seeing him again but decided to give him a chance. I found out that I have an older half-brother from his previous marriage. I'm glad he got in touch because he had changed, and we started a relationship. He passed away in 2020. We had a lot of years to be reacquainted, and I'm grateful for that. I had stayed in touch with Deana because I loved her, and I knew we could work things out. I went to Texas to be with her and we got married.

We had a daughter and named her Hailey. Some years later, we had twin girls, Reagan and Peyton. I sure love my family. Now if I find myself in a spiritual rut, it's because I haven't been praying in the spirit or reading the Bible.

This life is a constant struggle, a kind of tug-of-war between good and evil. Staying in Jesus, you can't help but get stronger and stronger.

THE TABLE OF LIFE

by Howard Baxla

As I sit here this morning in this old wooden chair that so many people have sat in and so few have respected, I realize I am so much like it is. I came into this world new and built by the hands of a great craftsman. He took a lot of care in making me. He shaped me just to the way he saw I needed to be, to do the job and complete the task. He covered me with a new skin, like cloth to make me stand out, yet to protect me. I was placed at the table of life with my two brothers and one sister. We made a complete set. We never worked together as one, but we were almost always around one another. Although one chair may have been removed from time to time, we still faced the table and did our job. Sometimes I would be used for other task, like giving someone a step up in life, which I always felt good about. I would be needed then, maybe not for the proper purpose, but needed. Kids have climbed on me, rocking us back and forth. I was honored to be there for them.

The elderly has used me for a leaning pole or to steady their weight and I was good with this as I was strong, being made very well. I was abused by many too, as they laid me back on my two legs, rocking me hard sometimes into the ground. I held my own, though, no matter what life gave me, I sported it and gave my all to it. There have been so many things in my life that has tried to break me, but I've held strong for the group called my family. I have a family of my own now. I look across the table of life, and I see a beautiful chair there now helping me to hold onto this set of four. The two young chairs need to know a lot about this rough life and how to do the job that that their great craftsman has built them for. I feel the need to take care of them and to help them be strong in this hard world. When there is a job to do that beats up on us, I want to be at the front for them so they won't bear the scars that I show. I want to hold up as long as I can to keep this group of four together, with hopes that I might one day see my little ones go out and become new sets of their own. As for me, I hope to one day sit with the beautiful chair that chose this life with me and look off into life's now fading table and see what it was that we had accomplished for our master craftsman.

MARANDA

The desire came to me strongly from the Holy Ghost to share my spiritual life story. I will do my best to tell it as and how it all happened. I hope this chapter that was written by me, Maranda, will be meaningful and heartfelt.

The first experience was when I was six years old, then again when I was nine years old being when I gave my heart and soul to my savior Jesus Christ and was baptized in water, later the baptism of the Holy Spirit, if that is not enough; I would like to share with you what happened as I was new to the spirit world, and it was something I did not understand at the time, but I knew it was from God, but what would other people think about this if mentioned to someone other than my sister, Beth, or my mother, Frances, or daughter Janice, or sons, Robert, Eugene, or Michael called Eli. No one other than some of my family would consider me sane, as I spoke of such things, or would understand. That was what I realized in the early 1970s. They keep these matters in "the closet," so I was told and as I learned this on my own.

My first experience was in 1953 and continued through all these seventy-three years of my life. Being led by the Spirit and having God's grace makes life a better place while on this sinful dwelling we call earth; at one time, it was filled with beauty and peaceful love. The magnificent part of being here is to have God looking after us as his children and having his angels in charge of our needs and safety; most of all to experience the love of Jesus Christ.

This book is truly a book of God, his manifestations of living with his children, what he has done for our family and me. Showing signs, he has shown us, miracle's that he performed, healing of our bodies, about angels we have seen, and demons that thought they would win and were disappointed. The ones that follow Jesus (faithful and dodge sin) and truly have a one-on-one relationship with Jesus and filled with his Holy Spirit shall see their prayers answered, see miracles, and receive miracles, shall see visual visions or visions in dreams. God wants all to know how much he loves everyone and wants us to be ready for his coming, which will be soon. Hell is a real place that was created for Satan and his fallen angels, but later had to be enlarged because of man's sinning.

Being six years old and learning how to manipulate a pencil with a piece of paper took too much practice and patience. Although my parents were more equipped with patience that was needed. But what was really giving me the biggest problem was to balance a stick with a pointed lead was harder than learning to write because there was a wart in that very same spot. So my parents told me they knew someone that they thought could help us. My heart lifted when I heard those words.

The next day, this young tall man came to visit. Mother introduced me to him and tells me he is a minister, and he would like to see the wart on my hand. Opening my hand so he could take a complete view, he says, "Do you believe Jesus can take this wart off your hand?"

"Sure I do," I said.

He took his large hand and cupped my hand inside. And then he prayed for Jesus to remove my wart, to relieve all discomfort for Maranda. Then still holding my hand, he told me, "I am going to wrap this small hankie of your Mother's around your hand." He made sure it was fitted perfect and asking if it was comfortable, he was telling me, "Don't look at your wart for two days and don't think about it and Jesus will remove it from your hand so you can write with no hurt, no discomfort."

Being certain to follow all instructions, trusting and having faith in my Lord Jesus Christ was what I was going to do.

Bruce, my daddy, says, "Guess what, Maranda, your two days are up. Would you like to look at your hand?"

"Yes! Yes!" I said.

So Mother slowly and carefully removed her little hankie, and I was eagerly looking. Mother turned to Daddy and said, "Bruce, God has removed it, just as we asked of him."

It was not in the hankie either. God had completely taken it away. This is a childhood memory that was always with me, and I have believed this was my pathway to Jesus building my faith in God. That was many years ago, before doctors really knew about the treatment as they do today for warts. Thank you, Jesus!

Now writing was a pleasure and enjoyment for the first time. And now I have patience also. But, most of all, at the age of six, I learned the most important lesson of all. That Jesus Christ is my healer.

When I was nine years old, Daddy, Mother, Beth, and my brother Powell and I, Maranda were on the third row of front seats of a small country church. I was the elder of the four children. My sister Cynthia had not been born at this time.

This was Easter Sunday, so the topic of the pastor's sermon was all about our savior Jesus Christ and what he had sacrificed for us. My focus was continually on the pastor's words. In my heart was always a special place for Jesus Christ. All of a sudden, tears came down my cheeks, I could not stop crying; my heart was broken from hearing all that Jesus had done for us and all that he went through, just for us, so we could one day go to heaven and be with him. About that time, I felt Mother put her arms around me and asked me, "What is wrong?"

All I could say was, "I don't know." (At that age, I did not know how to express my emotions) "Are you okay?" she asked, and my reply was, "My heart hurts." Now the pastor said to everyone, "Let's sing that graceful song, 'In the Garden.'" I felt a link was made between Jesus and me as they sang that song. It still is just as special now to me. To think that he gave his life for me, so I could have everlasting life to live in a city of Gold, to live with Jesus. As soon as the song began, the tears became stronger, and I was not crying now; I was bellowing. Mother asked me if I wanted to give my heart to Jesus. Yes! I gulped.

"That if thou confess with thy mouth the Lord Jesus and shall believe in thine heart that God hath raised him from the dead, thou shall be saved" (Rom. 10:9 KJV). I don't remember too much about what was said after that; I just remember being hugged and led out to the car. Arrangements were made for me to be water baptized in a couple Sundays.

"He that believeth and is baptized shall be saved, but he that believeth not shall be dammed" (Mark 16:16 KJV).

I would like to share this song, "In the Garden," written by Charles A. Miles, 1913.

> I come to the garden alone.
> While the dew is still on the roses,
> And the voice I hear falling on my ear
> The Son of God discloses.
> Refrain:
> And he walks with me, and he talks with me,
> And he tells me I am his own;
> And the joy we share as we tarry there,
> None other has ever known.
> He speaks, and the sound of his voice
> Is sweet and the birds hush their singing, and the
>   melody that he gave to me
> Within my heart is still ringing.
> I'd stay in the garden with him,
> Though the night is around me falling,
> But, he bids me go, though the voice of woe
> His voice to me is calling

Each day, I waited to be baptized was full of anticipation. While sitting on my backyard swing, wearing my new dress with a red-pleated skirt and a black bodice full of spaced colorful dots, which I would wear every day if Mother would allow, but I knew better. Glancing over the yard and seeing the huge mimosa tree that was across the driveway from our house, I was thinking, Jesus is so higher up in the sky than the huge tall tree. I yearned to be as close to Jesus as I could, and the more I thought about it, the more I wanted that closeness.

So running to the tree as fast as my little legs would carry me, getting there and looking up at the tree, I had no idea how I would climb this monster, but I the configuration completely has left my memory, but with no fear, my legs carried me to the lowest limb, which was about five or six feet high. Up, higher I climbed, until I could not climb anymore without feeling safe. I can still see the beautiful view from the enormous limb, and it made me feel so near Jesus, sitting there in the nice breeze looking up and talking to Jesus for a long time.

Unfortunately, that was the end of my climbing trees as soon as Daddy heard of it; he did not want his little girl to get hurt. So I agreed because Mother said Jesus was everywhere and he sees all we do (she drilled us on that in a nice way), so he is always near, so I was content with that. Finally the day came that I had been waiting for. I was so excited and a little nervous. This is a big step. There were some others to be baptized the same day. As I emerged into the water and coming up out of the water, I felt so holy; I felt like a feather, my heartfelt light and airy. I tried so hard to live for Jesus every day. When I was tempted, I would ask myself, *What would Jesus do if he were in my situation?*

Temptations come to us at all ages. Soon after being baptized, my teacher at school had asked for volunteers to collect for the March of Dimes. I was not anxious to volunteer because I thought of going to strangers' doors, and I was shy. Besides, my sibling and I were told not to talk to strangers. With some urges from classmates telling me how helpful it will be for those in needs, and besides there always are two of us together at each door. Not to mention our teacher tells us there would be a nice gift for the pair to collect the most dimes. So I gave in…so here we go.

Most people did not like strangers approaching their doors, I assume. Considering we had only two people to answer the doorbell or knock that we so heartily gave while walking in the heat of the day. The first person that answered the door was very friendly and asked us in, but we replied we were told not to go in anyone's home.

She smiled and said, "Please wait here, I think I have a few dimes." She filled half of one of the cards. We each were given one. We both thanked her and started all over again. As we were walking from one place to the other, my partner said, "You know what, the school does not know how many dimes we collect. We could just tell them we did not get any dimes, and we can split these we collect."

I did not want any part of that and told her that would be wrong the people need the collection. The next door was another nice lady; she had a few dimes she donated. As soon as she closed the door and we walked from the steps, my partner repeated what she said before. I told her that was stealing, and I do not want any part of it. So I gave her my card and told her she could have them both, and she could decide what she should do. I went home. I never said anything to my teacher. I felt that issue was between my partner and Jesus. Jesus is our judge.

Another time when I was four years old, Daddy was a butcher in the Red & White grocery store just a few blocks from our home. There was a crowd collecting in front of the store, our neighbor said. Mother, being concerned for Daddy, took me with her to see if he was in the building or not. She asked me to wait outside in front of the store. Well, while she was inside, a little girl younger than me came to me and said, "Look here at this bubblegum machine. Oh, look here, it is so hot it melted all the gumballs." And at that moment, she discovers the pennies will flow freely out of the machine.

She quickly collected all she can in her hands, in her pockets, and in her apron. She gladly told me to get some, and we can go next door and buy balloons that we can shape into animals. Always being told, "Jesus sees all we do." So I tell her, "Thank you for the offer but I don't think so." I did not want any part of stealing.

"Oh, they don't care, come on. I'll buy you some balloons at the drugstore." She couldn't get the drugstore door open, so I helped her open the door so she wouldn't hurt herself. The man behind the counter told me to enter the store. I did not need to stand outside until the fire was put out. Obeying my elders, I did as he requested. As soon as she was in the door, she raced to the counter where she starts emptying her pockets and reaching up, pushing the pennies on top of the counter to pay the man behind the counter. He asked if she broke her piggy bank to get all these pennies. She told him they came out of the hot bubblegum machine. He asks her if she touched anything hot, and if she was all right. She answered quickly, "Oh no," then right away she got down to business and explained she wanted the balloons that make the shape of animals and picking out her colors.

She said to the man, "Give her some too."

I explained, "I do not want any, sir." So she had all the balloons she wanted and the man said the fire truck just left so we could leave now. The little girl was leaving a long trail of balloons behind her. Looking for Mother as she was supposed to come back for me, I did not see her anywhere and I did not know what to do but to go home. As soon as I got the door open good, here came Mother. She was angry. I've never seen her like this. I was frightened. She grabbed a belt and started giving it to me on my sitting-down place. I was more heartbroken than ever because I did nothing wrong. Then she asked me questions and I told her what happened. She said, "You sit right her until I get back."

"Yes, ma'am."

It was about ten minutes later. Mother returned, and she was in tears. She said she spoke to the grocery manager and the druggist, "And they both said you did not take anything. I am so sorry I did not believe you." And I am happy to hear that Daddy was not in the store during the fire and no one was hurt, but they did have need to replace a large section of the store. That was the one and only spanking I had in my entire life. Mother always showed us how to love and respect each other, and I could always talk to her about anything. I felt so blessed.

Her mother (my grandmother) who lived not too far away came to care for me and now also my new sister Beth for Mother and Daddy to work. Children were mostly told to play outside during those years, and most of us really enjoyed it. My grandmother I called Grandma would make it so exciting. Some occasions, I was given old pie pans and shown how to make a mud pie like Mother makes her pies for supper. Sitting on the top step and holding my fresh made mud pie, I dropped a few drops on my dress and I had to run inside and show Grandma because I did not like to be dirty at all when I was young.

Just as I stood up, there was a pain in my foot. Oh my, I was crying; it hurt so badly. Grabbing the nail as I went in the door, Grandma was holding open for me. She said it will be all right; she was praying in between talking to me and as she was cleaning the wound. Always reassuring me, it is okay; there is nothing to worry about. When I hear her say this, I know Jesus will make it better, and she was a midwife that helped all around her farm and never charged for her service; most repaid her with things she may have need of. Grandma almost raised me until I was about five years old and off and on after five. She was always with me while Mother was training to be a mother to me (so Mother told me), and when my parents were at work, so I have a lot of Grandmother's understanding.

Several years later, I came in and said I had nothing to do outside (my age now was nine years old) and then she filled kitchen bottles that once contained ketchup, mustard, or any glass bottle that could hold water. There were no affordable plastic bottles at that time. She dropped a few drops of food color in each bottle, giving me a variety of beautiful colors. She said, "Put these in your bicycle basket and ride up and down the sidewalk in the sun and watch the colors. That made me happy, and now I had something to put in my new bicycle basket; I was excited. Of course I was instructed to ride slow and gentle, not to break the pretty colorful bottles. So gently I go up and down the sidewalk, and I felt like I was just given a new Rolls-Royce. She was right; the colors were so radiant and exciting, glistening in the sun. Such amazement! But of course that was my last fun with bottles; Daddy thought it wasn't safe, especially if I fell from my bike. They just did not know what bliss of joy it gave me.

Years had passed; now being fourteen, things seem to be changing in our families. My favorite aunt that used to have me visit a couple weeks when school was out for summer came for my usual stay with her. She lived in the country in South Carolina and so did we at that time, but it was many miles apart. She didn't mind; she loved to have a child at her home. She also took turns with me and her niece on her husband's side of the family; her name was Marie. Marie and I were about four years apart in age, her being the older of the two of us. We did not get to see each other very much because her mother had a severe disease and was in and out of hospitals, and Marie wanted to spend all the time she could with her mother.

Feeling the same way if it was my mother in her condition, Marie and her mother seemed to have a very close and loving relationship. She had a younger sister, but I don't remember meeting her. My Uncle Jim had a small country store down the road from their house where I was visiting, but he usually would be there all day unless he needed something he left in his office, which was in the backyard building or leave and go into town where his other store was located; it had a large red circle on it. I never was allowed to go to his stores, having a lot of love for my aunt, but it seemed we had a bit of communication problem. She worked in a clothing store long hours on her feet selling ladies clothes; she had been promoted to a higher position. I'm thinking her title was supervisor. She kept me in nice school clothes. Being alone all day until she came in, I sure was happy to see her. First thing she does is make something with a can of biscuits and make something to go with it and after eating; quickly, she begins making her foot soak and then with her feet in the container she turns on the *Doris Day Show*, and we would watch it while her feet are soaking. Then it is time for bed.

She was blessed with a son who was much older than myself, not sure how much older, but to me, he looked almost like a daddy figure to me; I've only seen him once while during all the years I visited in their home. He never came in the house either when I was there; almost forgot he existed.

I was alone, unless Marie dropped in, and she came that day, I was feeling lonesome, and she showed me where there was a very large sword, and she took it out and said we can have fun with this, but we have to be careful with it and make sure to put it back. So this was a long sword that was to wrap around your waist and hang along your leg for fighting. We were taking turns sliding the material strap around our waist and walking a small area to get the feel of it. The sword was so pretty; it had all kinds of deigns and colorfulness on it. Marie said it was okay, and she was there more than me, so I trusted her judgment. Oh boy, I finally had something to carry on conversation with my aunt tonight when she comes home. That did not work out the way it was planned.

About the time I explained the happy event, she let me know right away that was not a toy, and we knew better than to touch anything in the outside building. Oh my goodness, that sure did backfire. Well, nothing else to talk about this night. I did learn that the sword was an antique and very valuable weapon that was used in war. Oh my…

The next day, Aunt told me there was a friend of hers that she has known for years that her daughter was about my age and they (her mother and my aunt) thought it would be nice for us to spend some time together. "Well, okay," I said. Well, this was something I was doing because she wanted it. Being shy and bashful like I was and a little nervous about meeting her, the phone rang the next day, and this girl said her name was Nancy and my aunt said she could call and talk to me. Having a phone call first made me relaxed and the new conversation was going well. Then she told me her mother gave her permission to double date, but she needed another girl to go with them. I had never been on any type of date. I didn't know what it was expected to be.

Right away, I tried to explain to her this was new for me, and I did not think I wanted to do this, but thank you for asking. Well, that did not satisfy her; she would not stop until I said okay. The only reason I said yes was because I did not want to insult my aunt to her friend. Since my aunt knew them well for so long, I thought it would be okay; even though I was scared to go. So I was taken to meet Nancy at her home, and no one was there but Nancy. My aunt dropped me off and leaves. I rang the doorbell, and Nancy answered the door, very excited. "Come on in, and I will call the guys and tell them all is clear. What did she mean? Well, here comes the "guys" in a convertible Impala. My first thoughts were *Oh no, my hair!* (teenager thoughts), so I pulled out a scarf with large dots and placed it on my head and pull the corners under my ears and tie it behind my head. Of course, the backseat guy and I were assigned together. Feeling so out of place, but trying to be nice and friendly; all of a sudden, the back seat guy looked at me and then hollered to the front seat as we traveled down the highway with the top down, "What is this thing on her head?"

Boy! I could have crawled out the car about that time. So I knew the scarf had to go: so yanking it off my head and healing no friendliness for this joker, my hair swirled and flew and stood up on my head while I am rubbing my face so I can see. I am just sitting there, hoping soon the ride would be over. Shortly, the ride was over, and I was wishing then that the wheels were still turning. Learning what this outing was all about: first, the front seat couple wrap into one and the signal gave the backseat guy the go ahead, but he was stopped just as he got started. I was taught that was for a husband and wife only. He was angry and told Nancy, "I thought you said she wanted to?" Well, God was watching over me because I was the stick in the mud and the driver started to drive and they took me home. Thank you, Jesus.

Soon after that, I was having excruciating stomach pain. My aunt just knew I needed laxative, even though I told her there was no problem there. The pain would move often and not getting better. So she called her brother (Bruce), and Daddy said bring her home, and we will see what we can do. They had a small meeting, and Daddy called the doctor and was told right away to take me to the hospital. There, I was taken right back to surgery for appendectomy. Everything was feeling much better after I was in the hospital room and the procedures were completed. Everyone was so attentive and a pleasant place to be, even though I would rather be at my comfy home with my family.

Once again, back to my healthy self again and back to my schedule of school and watching the three siblings before Mother and Daddy return from work. Mother usually was home about an hour after we were home from school. Things weren't as happy as it was when I was a child. For one thing, I missed my grandma; she was older now and lived some miles away so we visited when we could. Mother and Daddy had purchased a Jim Walter home that someone had built and lived in about a couple years and decided to sell. My parents said it was a great place with acres of land so Mother wanted new furniture, and it was fixed up rather nicely I thought. Daddy had just purchased a new push button Rambler automobile, and for some reason, my parents wanted me on a bike before I could walk, and now they want me behind the wheel of a car; now that I am fourteen, they seem to think it is a must for some reason.

Then the days became dreary; Mother and Daddy were not close any more, and it reflected on us kids. They were back lashing each other and trying to keep it away from us kids as much as possible. Mostly, it was Daddy accusing Mother of men where she worked. And my daddy that I love dearly climbed the oil drum outside the bathroom window, and Mother heard the noise and ran around the outside of the house and called him down. He told her he wanted to see what he had made. I happened to be in the bathroom tub and covering myself as I heard the noise. It was hard enough to be a teenager, but it is harder to live in situations that are unavoidable. I feel sorry for Mother because I know somehow (different ways) she was being abused.

Mother told me one day to go to the store and get her a loaf of bread. I told her I really did not want to drive the car, it made me nervous, but she insisted and said I would be fine. She gave the directions where the turns were and it was about twenty miles one way. So after a quick demonstration on how the car operated, I made the journey with no problem, but as I entered the store I was asked if my parents knew I was driving out in country roads. I replied, "Yes" in embarrassment and thanked them for the bread I just purchased. The cashier brought it to my attention that police cars do check these roads for driver's license. Thinking it over, most kids would probably be happy or feel proud about doing what I just did, but some of us like to get a good feel of things before jumping in. Yes, that is who I am.

It was not long Daddy had attacked Mother in the dining room, and she was pleading for him to stop as he had her on the floor. That was a fearful, shocking moment. My siblings were crying and afraid; I knew I had to do something I was the oldest child. We were eating at the table when this happened and not thinking; jumping to my feet, my hand reached for the paper-thin aluminum coffee pot sitting on the table, and Daddy was feeling it on his head. Thank God for that expulse reaction; it calmed things down. Of course, now Daddy knew I felt he was at fault so I knew I was not going to be in his favor. Next morning, he demanded me to iron his shirt for work. Mother had already left for work. He loudly told me, "Your mother won't iron my shirt and it's time you learn." Well, doing my best with tears rolling down my cheeks, he grabbed the shirt and said, "Get away from here. I'll do it myself." That was the last time I saw Daddy for a long time.

That afternoon, Mother wanted me to go to the store again and thinking in a daze as the car took me down the lonesome country road my mind running full of all the things going on around our lives, deciding that this life was not for me and did not want to go back to it. So the car keep going, and soon it came to Columbia South Carolina where the car just keep going and going. Then seeing the gas gauge, thinking gas might be needed soon, what am I to do? Just then the large fair grounds were full of all types of rides, and it was dusk dark so it was closing for the night. I don't know where my courage came from, but walking up to the open gate and walking through, a man came my way and said they are closing for the night. "You need to come back tomorrow and have a good time."

Then explaining to him my car tank is almost empty so a job was what I needed. He asked me where my car was so I pointed and described it to him. Then he asked, "Do your parents know where you are?" After telling him, I had to leave home and I needed time to think. He said, "Well, do you think you could sell tickets and be comfortable talking to people?" He said for me to come with him; he was so nice and feeling that he could be trusted I followed along. We were at a loud wild sounding group of men in one room (but I was outside the door with the man he did not want me to go inside), drinking and playing cards. Right away, they started asking about me, and right away, he settled them down and told the guys, "Hands off. She will be her tomorrow to sell tickets and no one was to go to the ticket booth."

They all said they agreed and he looked at one guy individually and said, "Especially you, John."

John nodded and said, "I understand." As we left, he explained his name was Rusty, and if I needed anything, he would be close by; he showed me a box truck and said that is where he stays, "But you can stay here tonight, you won't be safe in your car. He continues telling me it was clean and there is a mattress on the floor and it has clean sheets and covers. I think you will find it comfortable." He promised without my saying or questioning anything that he will lock the door as soon as I entered the truck and he would not open it until the morning and I will let you know it is me first." The Lord God was with me again; later in my life and looking back, it was a miserable thought at all the misfortunate things that could have occurred at that episode in my life.

Thank you, my Heavenly Father, for the protection of the Holy Spirit. Of course I had no clue that God was over seeing my path way during my early days of my life, but he was because there was so many chances that harm was facing me or death at times. I was like the young walking blind and seeing no harm. After Rusty opened the truck, he was standing outside and was telling me he was going to work and he would show me where I could work. This being my first real job, I had confidence that I could do this as he explained. "The customer will tell you how many tickets they want, you count them off the roll and tell them how much it is and after receiving the money you give them the tickets and change."

Honestly, I think I was working a dead fair, I mean two people came to my booth and no one else and I noticed the guys were taking the rides apart and packing them up. Seeing that this nice guy, Rusty had done so much for me; I was ready to leave and I told Rusty and thanked him for all he did. He asked me where I would go. So I replied, I am not sure but I will be okay. So he pulled out a few dollars for my pay for gas and told me to be careful. I thanked him again for being so nice and helpful. Back on the road again and having no idea where to go, there was no phone at home so I could not call Mother, and I did not want Mother to worry about me so I thought I would go to the police department. I know they will help me. Parking the car on the main street of Columbia was scary because the only parking spot was on a steep hill. I never parked like this and on top of that I am going to the police surely they will look at the car I drove so it has to be parked correctly. After parking and pushing the door as hard as I could to open the door to get out was not easy for me, but I managed.

Checking my parking and seeing it was so good, it surprised me. Walking into the police station, there sat a policeman at a desk and he spoke to me asking who I was, "What can I do for you?" Well, I told him I ran away from home and I have no place to go. He wants to know how I got to the police department. Telling him the car was parked outside he had another policeman to check it out and that was how they located my parents. Making it clear to them I did not want to see my daddy. He said, "Do you have family or friends you can stay with?"

"Yes, sir, my aunt."

He said, "Have a seat. This will take a while."

Not knowing phone numbers where my parents worked or my aunt's phone number was no help. (No cells then.) He said, "Your parents will need to be notified before we can send you anywhere." Of course they had already called Mother from the information on the car registration but not telling me yet. Finally after a couple hours of waiting, this is what I was told.

"You say you don't want to go home so no one will force you to go home, but your aunt cannot come now but maybe a little later."

My heart dropped. "Well, where should I go?" I asked.

"There is a place where other runaways are kept until you find a place to stay."

My thoughts while I was waiting were if others are having the same problem maybe they would understand and be nice. Now the greatest site of all here is Mother; I was so happy to see her. I could see worry and hurt on her face, and I knew her heart was crying. I wanted so much to be with her and my sisters and my only little brother, but not with fussing and fighting. Thinking of my siblings knowing they will be fine because they were young and Daddy always treated them with love because they were so young. Mother was asking me to come home, and I explained I just can't live like that; it is not good. She said she would find us a home and she will come for me as soon as she has things settled for us to have our own place just Mother and the children. But for right now, I would have to go to the reform school until my aunt could come for me and shortly after that we would all be together, just Mother and her children.

No clue did I have about a place like that. But I learned fast. Mother had brought my clothes, toiletries, and my razor for shaving my legs, which I was adamant about. They would not let me see or talk to Mother. This made me sad; it was like I was being punished even though I tried so had to be an upright person. Then the woman in charge brought me in a room with just the two of us, and she had my little suit case on the desk with wired fence surrounding the room around us. I felt like a caged animal as she went through her procedure of going through my suitcase, which I was not allowed to touch. She picked out what she wants me to have and what she doesn't; picking up my little handle of my stick razor she says, "You will not be allowed this."

I said, "Please I use it every day."

Her reply was "Not here." I never looked at it as being a weapon but she did. So I sat around by myself and waited for Mother to come or my aunt after making my bed and then sitting on it, where I stayed all day except for meals. I had to go to cafeteria; that was one of the rules. I was the saddest person in there, and I had no energy to make friends or be sociable. The other girls in my room (there were three of them) were talking about me where I could hear them. One tried talking to me, but I did not feel like making friends; I was stressed. So the one says, "You have to watch out for the quite ones." Guessing they will leave me alone now and they did.

I was there for two weeks before my aunt came for me, and she explained that this is just a temporary thing. So here I am going nowhere, still floating, but it was nice of her, and being young, I had no idea how it affected her to drop all and take on my problem. Never hearing from Nancy again, which, I guess is a blessing, she was wild and I was not. I told my aunt about the double date when I came home that day; it seemed to upset her so I never mentioned it again and neither did she. She was, of course, back to her job every day except Sunday, and Uncle Jim was at the country store every day. To my surprise, Uncle came home and in the house; I was surprised. He went to his bedroom, which is next to the room I sleep in. He said he was going to rest for a while so I said I will be quite so you can rest.

It was just a few minutes he called me in his bedroom. I stood at the doorway looking in and answered him. He said, "Come here, I have something to tell you." So I walked halfway across the room. He then told me I had to come closer so I could hear him. My knees were knocking at this point, but he was my uncle. I had to obey him. As I got to his bed he said, "Sit down on the side of the bed." I eased my body down on the side as he was in the middle of the bed. He quickly came over and ran his arm across one of my breast. I jumped up quickly and ran in the living room, scared to death. He got up and left. Well, what do I do now? That I am afraid of my uncle, feeling I cannot stay here, but how in the world do I go about explaining this to my aunt?

Today happened to be the day she said I could get off of the school bus at the downtown drugstore and have a Coke float at the soda shop and then walks down to her work place and we would head to her house. Not knowing any of the kids that hung out at the soda shop it was still nice to be there, and I did have a few conversations with some of them. After what Uncle did, I knew I could not stay there if he wanted to fondle or if he just wanted me to go. Either way, it meant I could not stay there. My mother always understood when I would tell her things that affected me; I knew my aunt would also. I was very wrong; she said, "Maranda, I don't believe you."

That was like a slap in the face. So what happens now? She said, "I am taking you home as soon as I can, young lady." What could I say? My aunt called Mother and told her I am going back to Mother's and wanted to know how Mother's process of living arrangements was coming along. After their conversation, Aunt handed me the phone and said, "Your Mother wants to talk to you." Oh boy!

"Yes, Mother?"

She began to give me some good news. Well, my mother had been working hard for us and making away for us kids. She had gotten a legal separation from my dad and had gotten us an apartment in a housing project where we all would be happy together. But we could not move in for a week. So I hung out at Auntie's for a week. During that time, Uncle never came to the house while I was there, and Marie visited me, being somewhat part of the family and my friend I told her what Uncle had done. She said, "He did the same thing to me. He just does not want us here."

Reunited and in a loving family, my dad was not allowed to see us for some time, thinking about a year. When we have him over to visit us children, instead of spending time with us he sits proudly with his new wife-to-be, which he lets us know she had a hefty bank account, stocks, and bonds and a brand-new car paid for. I don't think he left out anything. She did have it all and she was an alcoholic, and she told him he had to save a thousand dollars within one year to prove he could handle money, and in that day and time, that was a sizeable sum. We were hungry more than not with usually having one eating a day, can't call it a meal. Usually serving a pot of beans that we nibble on for a couple of days or bologna sandwiches or hotdogs if we could afford the meat or mac and cheese, but no one complained; we knew Mother was doing the best she could and she always have food for us.

Becoming soon sixteen, my friend that I meet in school was dating and asked me to double date; of course I had my fill of double dating, but I would like to meet someone nice to talk to, spend some time with, maybe go to a movie. Not going on the double date and never feeling as if I should. My entertainment was walking. I loved to walk from where we lived to up town about four miles. I would stopped in a restaurant or drugstore and have a soda to take a rest before heading back on the trail.

Of course living in Columbia and the army base being located there means the town is loaded with army men. But being underage at that time, they would not touch someone classified as jail bait, so I talked to some of them as I would rest for the walk back home. Most that I talked to wanted to talk of their family and where they lived. Seems like they were homesick and some were boasters and loud mouths, so when this happened, it's time for me to go. Then I meet this guy that was from Florida; he was telling me what a beautiful place it was and how his Dad owned the largest auction barn in the county and his dad was an auctioneer. That was Greek to me, but it sounded good. He was polite and talked to my mother as much as he did to me. I was going to be sixteen in two weeks. He had recently turned twenty-one. He went to the PX on base and purchases a beautiful necklace for me and my mother. This was the setting to ask Mother for my hand in marriage, but I did not realize it at the time. We were driving around with the radio on and the song came on singing: "Going to the chapel and we're going to get married" (Chapel of Love). As this song was playing, he said to me, "Will you go to Texas with me?"

As I was playing with the radio knobs and still focusing on the radio, I replied, "Yes." He was excited, and he couldn't wait to ask my mother for my hand. Mother talked to me after he left and he was invited to come back the next night to get his answer. This was the year 1964, and the day we married was on my sister Beth's birthday. Mother was happy for me and she called her brother and her mother (Grandma) to come to the ceremony and also brought the preacher that was my mother's Sunday schoolteacher when she was young. They traveled over one hundred miles one way just to be there for my special day. This made me feel like I was surrounded by family that loved me for my wedding. They were all seated and waiting for me to come down the living room stairs, and I did not disappoint them, but I was not in a wedding dress. I had a beautiful yellow dress I had planned to wear, but it was not laundered in time with all the excitement so I picked out my olive green (remember, I was sixteen now, lol). Everyone was happy, full of joy and happiness for us, and made me feel happy; but I was a little concerned because I was leaving the only family I know to live with a stranger I knew for only two weeks to go meet his family in Florida and then to Killeen, Texas, where they had transferred him. He then took the ring he purchased and picked out and with instruction from the preacher, put it on my finger, and he gave me his ring that he also picked out and purchased for him, and I put it on his finger and everyone giving hugs and blessings and told us goodbye, and rice is falling from the air. We got in his car and he pulled off, and in a few feet, he says, "Your little brother is running behind the car and crying. Do you want me to stop?"

I said no, holding back the tears because I probably would have stayed, seeing him so upset. I could not handle it, and I regretted not stopping to give him one last hug for the rest of my life. My brother at that time was six years old.

The first place we went was to the uptown Columbia hotel, and he got the wedding suite because there was a convention in town and all other rooms were taken. That was the most frightening time because I had no idea what any man undressed was like, and I knew he wanted intimacy on his wedding night, what man would not. Suppose if there was love between us, I could respond and learn to enjoy being with him and the same for him, but it was too soon for me and another blessing I noticed it was my lady time of the month. So he went out for the essentials I needed and then we went asleep with me in my usual PJs of flannel cotton. I don't know what he slept in but I was on the other side of the bed.

The trip to Florida was a great trip; we stopped several places for road side attractions. This was so new to me and exciting to me and we got to know each other a little better. Getting to his mother and father's house, she made me feel welcome, but his dad acted as if I was a disease. Then she announced she wanted to see the marriage certificate before we slept together in her house. All of a sudden, I felt like a tramp for the first time, but thinking how she must feel, I just let that feeling go. After her verification of our honesty, we *were* allowed to stay in her home. They did have a nice home, nice furnishing, and they had the huge auction barn, just as my husband had said.

Okay, I was free from excuses, and it is bedtime. Oh my gosh! No, not in his parents' house and our room is next to each other and our doors are open; please, that was what I was saying inside… So while he was saying good night to them, I pretended I was sleeping. He came to bed and went to sleep. Next night, I tried the same thing; well, him thinking I am asleep, he goes to the tiny bathroom door between the bedrooms and called for his dad with a whisper, careful not to wake his mom. His dad came to the door and asked what was wrong. He began telling him he does not know what to do; she don't want to you know. His dad says, "She married you, didn't she? That makes her your wife, so she is yours."

My husband asked his dad, "What about Mom?"

His dad replied, "She takes a sleeping pill every night, don't worry about her. She won't wake up." So my husband forced himself on me, an uneducated virgin, and no feeling from him but lust. Next day, it hurt to walk, but I tried to pretend it didn't hurt and tried to hide my embarrassment from his family.

A week later, we left for Killeen, Texas. That was a long ride, and all the belonging we had was in the car with us. In Texas, he found a tiny apartment in Killeen. I was not allowed out of the house because we lived near but not on the army base, and he said I could be in danger when going out alone. I moved from an army base in Columbia, and I was not imprisoned there. I was going crazy not allowed out of the house. All doors had to stay locked. I reminded him about where I lived before, and he stood firm on his thoughts.

One day, after months of lockdown, I was going stir crazy. I confronted him with this again and he would not bend. Then I said I have to go for a walk. I need fresh air, so I went for a walk. I got about three blocks, and he discovered I was not there. Here came his car up beside me. "Get in the car," he said. Saying to him, "I have to go for a walk." Walking was something that was enjoyment for me, plus my body ached because I was locked in and had no exercise. So he stopped the car, jumped out of the driver seat, ran around the car, and grabbed me and threw me in the car. "I'll teach you to do what I tell you."

This was like a different man from the one I met. He was not kind in bed either, and he expected me to run to him as many times a day as he would like. This is no lie; he made all excuses he could to leave base to get home, and many times he leaves without a pass daily. Of course nothing was said to my mother because I was not allowed money or stamps. And there was not much food because he was on army pay, and the wife's allotment had not started as of yet and he was not good at managing what he had; of course, he was in charge of all.

There was a lady in the next-door apartment that had a little girl about three years old, and she was also pregnant. She came to my front door one day and seemed so nice and offered to teach me to knit, even giving me a skin of yarn and needles. That really helped with my locked in time I was serving. Then she came over another time and asked me if I would like to go with her shopping. I sure would but I am not allowed by my husband to go anywhere. "Oh come on, you will be with me. I go out often and no one bothers me, come on."

She did not need to say that twice I was more than ready to and I liked being with her and her little girl; she was so pretty and sure was a good child. Oh, how nice it was to go in a store and look around again. We talked about size, color, wishes, and wants, just having a good time. Then we headed for home, and I helped her unload the shopping bags, which weren't very much. As we get into her apartment, she started pulling things out of the front of her maternity skirt; it was unreal: newborn clothes, dish clothes, you name it. I did not have any idea this was going on, and I was standing beside her the whole time in the store. She offered me some of her prizes, but I turned them down. That was the last of our friendship. As soon as my husband heard that I had been out of the house, he jumped up and headed next door when the man was home to tell him I was not to go on outings.

He came back into the house a while later with a big grin on his face and told me I know how to pick friends because the husband was a much higher rank than my husband was. So there was no more said about that and our neighbors were transferred to another state two days later. My husband had asked for return trip to Germany after he had finished his tour and enjoyed it so much he put in for another before I met him, so now he wanted me to go to Germany, my first trip from South Carolina, my home state was when I met him. He told me, in Germany where he will be, they go to the store and shop for their food daily because there is no refrigeration there, but some places have electricity. Since he was going to Germany, he had a leave coming before he made his journey. So this was our first time to leave Killeen, a small town I lived in but never seen.

Of course he wanted to go to his mother's to have time there before he leaves. We were there about a couple months, and then he took me to my mother's home. By the way, my mother had now purchased a beautiful brick home with a full basement, which was made into a nice bedroom and nice bath; she said I could lodge in it while I was there. Waiting for my timing to get my required shots before transporting to Germany, the base would let me know when to come for them. Meanwhile my husband was in Germany, and I was thinking of getting a job somewhere but I had no experience or reference and still sixteen. I was receiving the ninety-nine-dollar allotment a month from the army. If the money was carefully calculated, it would make me through the month. Days with my mother were happy and pleasant; she had a good nature. Somehow she had bought or required a large guinea pig that was allowed to run lose around the house. They trained him to come running to the refrigerator each time the door was opened. It was so funny; he always makes the loud squeal on his trip to the refrigerator and running so fast that he skids around the side of the room making his turn.

Grandma was not very fond of him. Being happy for my mother but not knowing how long she would own that beautiful house because of the night activity. My grandma was there when I came, and I was so happy to see her but she did not stay long. She said she could not sleep because of the ghost at night was what she called them. It was demons that were in the house from the previous owner as was my understanding in later life after the filling of the Holy Ghost. The previous owner had a child to drown in the bathtub and some of the neighbors thought the mother brought harm to the child. While I was in the basement and I slept hard and I am not afraid of noises so nothing bothered me, but the rest could not sleep because of the moving furniture in the living room. Mother was getting ready to relocate. The attic fan would come on and off whenever it wanted during the night; only at that time, we did not know how to command demons to leave and could not without the power of the Holy Ghost.

The more I thought of the country of Germany, I decided I did not want to be in a country I cannot speak the language plus the difficulty of utilities; also, it was necessary for me to have shots before I could go. I took the first booster and decided to stick to my guns. No go! He can't pick me up and throw me in the airplane. So I wrote my husband a letter and told him how I felt. It was not long he sent me a letter stating he is getting a discharge from the army, and he is coming to get me soon. And he did.

Taking me to Florida and he worked with his dad for a while, also with other jobs. Jobs were so easy to come by at that time, and for some reason, he was never employed for a long. This was the end of the year 1965, and I was told I was I was with child, which made me happy. I just knew I was going to have a little girl; believe it or not, they had no way of telling the mother for sure what gender the child would be. But I knew I was going to have a girl. My mother-in-law chuckled and said, "I can't see that happening." Not really knowing what she meant but just overlooking her expression. I surprised them all when my precious little girl was born, and then I was told that for many generations no girls were born to my husband's family. I named her after both her grandmothers.

After some years passed, this family life was not like I thought it should be. My husband was hardly ever home, and I did have my children to love and share my life, but I still was not allowed to drive or walk anywhere that was for pleasure or entertainment. I knew no one in Florida, but his parents and my mother. And I had my hands full being a mother and wife now twenty-four years old.

Once a week, I was allowed to shop for groceries; shopping with such a small amount of money we could hardly eat, also taking the children with me, which I had two beautiful boys thirteen months apart. They were always as close as twins and still are today. When I was pregnant with my daughter, I was left at home because it was not safe for me to travel many miles so my husband went to South Carolina and got my mother and grandma to be with me and helped her find an apartment in Tampa, Florida, and we were in a small town about fifty or sixty miles away. He really liked my mother probably because they always seem to communicate well. It was comfort to have her in the same state, but I was not allowed to make a long-distance call, the only reason I had a phone was because it was in the house when he bought it, and it was a very old phone and my husband liking antiques he let it stay… Not being able to use the car to go see Mother and she had no automobile and so it was almost as if she was still in South Carolina. But the joy of having Mother with me at the hospital as I gave birth to my first child was a wonderful feeling.

My sister Beth's husband was not so good to her either. We seldom saw each other she was strapped with rules and limitations almost like me. So I decided to learn to make things that the children needed. I couldn't go and buy them clothes because that would cause me to handle money and only my husband would do that. His mother would buy their clothes and toys and bring them or send them to the children, but I felt it would be nice if I could give my children something. This made a close bond between the children, my husband, and his mother, but it made me see that it left a distance between the children and myself. This desire arose from a piece of fabric that his mother sent to me from the auction along with an old singer sewing machine. It made the nicest hanging diaper shelf. At that time, the green stamp catalog was passed out freely to grocery stores for the customers to look through the catalog to pick their desired gift you could acquire by turning in the green stamps you saved from shopping. In the catalog were the exact size measurements for the pictured diaper shelf. Other items of my sewing products was a nice country bonnet for my daughter and a doll that was small enough to sit in her little hand, not to mention how relaxing it was for me as the items were created. For my sons, they had matching shirts and pants made for them. I thank the Lord for helping me make the old country bonnet; this was how we located our daughter at a flea market when she was lost in the crowd.

Then good news arrived in a letter, my sister Beth, five years younger than me, will arrive soon for a visit. That was a wonderful surprise now I can meet her son and have some time with her it has been so long since we have visited. After her welcome and some conversation, she could hardly wait to tell me her good news. She explained that she had received the Holy Ghost and continued to explained how and where with all the details. I did not understand most of what she was saying since it was all new to me. I knew Father, Son, and Holy Ghost and to me that just described the God head; I received it all, I thought, the day I claimed Jesus as my savior and baptized in water. With Bible opened, she was following me around as I cooked or picked up around the house. I thought she was off the deep end. This was some strange stuff. You say you speak with other tongues when you pray? You say the Holy Ghost you have I can have also? I had to think about this. This sounds like witchcraft to me.

But she is reading from the Kings James Bible. This is scary. This is my sister; she wouldn't lie to me. I had all these things going through my mind. After the children went to bed, she asked me to pray with her. She tried so much in a kind way to encourage me; she realized how important this was for salvation, but I did not have a clue. She explained to me in such a loving way how important this is and how much we are missing without being baptized in the Holy Spirit. So I agreed, but I still did not understand all she was saying. She put her arm around me and was trying to hold back her tears and explained how much she loved me and wanted me to have all that God has to offer us. Jesus let me feel his love and tenderness so I knew for sure this was Jesus. I felt his love so strong. Then going around in my mind was, all she reads and talks about is in the KJV Bible (at that time all I knew of Bibles was the one that was guarded on the coffee table which was a KJV Bible when we were young), it is not her word but God's Word I am hearing.

As I began to listen, I felt a tug on my heart again, but still it was not total surrender. That night, we were praying, and she said to me do you want to receive the Holy Ghost? Through tears and loss of voice and emotions, I nodded my head, yes. I understand and that is what I am going to do. I made up my mind that Jesus was going to be my life. I prayed to Jesus and telling him I surrender all for him, expecting to be filled with the Holy Ghost. We began calling Jesus's name and praising Him. She laid her hands on me to receive as we said, "Jesus, Jesus, Jesus" over and over, faster and faster. Jesus is the one that brings the Holy Ghost. After about fifteen minutes, the Holy Ghost fell on me, and I was filled with his spirit. I was filled because as it happened—not with my strength, but His, I very fast, leaped up from my seat to standing and jumping, and one word came from my mouth. It was the word *hod-gee*. Surprised at what had just taken place and the way I was feeling, feeling holy, pure. Now realizing I just received the baptism of the Holy Ghost and spoke in the heavenly language. Everybody receives in a different way is what I have heard; maybe because God makes us all different.

> John answered, saying unto them all, I indeed baptize you in water; but one mightier than I cometh, the latchet of whose shoes I am not worthy to unloose: He shall baptize you in the Holy Ghost and with fire. (Luke 3:16 KJV)

> Who, when they were come down, prayed for them, that they might receive the Holy Ghost: (For as yet he was fallen upon none of them: only they were baptized in the name of the Lord Jesus.) Then laid they their hands on them, and they received the Holy Ghost. (Acts 8:15–17 KJV)

> God is a Spirit: and they that worship him must worship him in spirit and truth. (John 4:24 KJV)

I was reborn with so much to learn; that was fifty years ago, believe me, God has shown us and taught us a lot since we received the Holy Ghost. The next morning after I received the Holy Ghost, Beth and I are one in Christ and we were so happy and full of joy. That is what God does for us; He sends the Holy Ghost to bring joy among other things.

But the fruit of the Spirit is love, joy, peace, longsuffering, gentleness, goodness and faith, Meekness, temperance: against such there is no law (Gal. 5:22–23 KJV).

After receiving the Holy Ghost; that was all we talked about and prayed together. God had brought a love between us that neither of us had known before, we thought we loved each other and always there for each other, but this was a deep holy love we found through the Holy Ghost. Beth tried to tell me everything she had learned at this time in her life about the Holy Ghost. She had received the Holy Ghost just a couple months ago, and she helped our younger sister to receive the Holy Ghost also, and many more throughout her life.

The next night, we prayed in my bedroom, rejoicing and praising Him for filling us with His Spirit. Tears of joy filled our eyes as I looked over to Beth I explained, "Your face, it is so white!" As she was pointing in amazement, she was describing the same on my face, and I was astonished! Then she pointed to the large mirror and said, "Look, let's look in the mirror." I could not help feeling leery and in awe, but anxious at the same time. Beth puts her arm around me and we go to the large mirror.

There I saw the circle of whiteness on our faces, but I could not see our faces for the whiteness; it was larger than our heads. Then the glow passed over our whole body, we became white as snow and glowing. What a site! We could still see everything except our faces were not visible while the light was there. I took it all in, looking in the mirror feeling like a stiff board because it was *something out of this world*. I being stunned and amazed taking this very serious and Beth was thrilled and excited and enjoying God's gift we were in gulped in at this special short time. But as long as we were watching ourselves and each other it was there for us. Beth said, laughing, "Watch." She swirled her arm around and the light on her arm made trails of light in the direction she moved her arm. God, I thought was delighting in our joy. I know we were and I could understand now and enjoy God's love to his children.

And he said unto them, Unto you it is given
to know the mystery of the kingdom of God: but
unto them that are without, all these things are
done in parables:

That seeing they may see, and not perceive;
and hearing they may hear, and not understand;
lest at any time they should be converted, and
their sins should be forgiven them. (Mark 4:11–
12 KJV)

Can you image how we felt? I never dreamed that we in the flesh could experience such spiritual things. The Bible clearly said, "God is spirit" and I can understand how He would use the spiritual events just as he did with Moses by splitting the Red Sea for them to cross over on the ground while the waters stood still up on both sides of the sea and standing still until they all passed. The disciples were unbelieving when Jesus came to them in the spirit after he rose from the dead. But they surely believed when he ate and drank with them and scared to prove it was indeed himself Jesus Christ. So after I studied my Bible more and more, the truth was opened to me. I understood what I was reading; it was not so much like a foreign language anymore.

Next day, tears of sorrow. Beth had to leave and my heart fell as soon as she left. I felt so sad. We had no idea when we would see each other again. There was no one else I knew that had this gift and could pray with me. It would be even a greater joy if our husbands would also except the Lord Jesus and live for him. I can only imagine what a holy reunion that may have been for my husband and me. But we all have our choices. God gives us choices he never forces anything on us. He asked for our love freely and we come as we are. We have no need to shine or sparkle to be presented to him before we are confessing our sins and accepting him for our Lord and savior. He loves us all. Come as you are and live in heaven. Oh, what a wonderful day that will be to enter his glory and live in the spirit. No more sickness, anger atmosphere, hunger, loneliness, and no more evil. Satan will be bound! Praise the Lord!

I was feeling so sad and sluggish this morning because my sister was not here today, and I think I was maybe still in a daze from the experience we shared yesterday. Sure gave me a lot to think about, especially after being filled with the baptizing of the Holy Ghost.

Laundry was waiting and the children wanted to go outside to play. They lifted my heart; God has many reasons for giving children. I am thinking one of them is giving us joy. Laundry day, they really enjoy because the laundry room was a small closet room in the opened carport. Yes, we lived in Florida and this is the lifestyle in Florida at that time in the early 1970s. Our yard was fenced in, but I felt complete if I was always outside with them. My sons had big wheels that they liked to ride to the gate and then bump into the gate, which causes the gate to bounce open. Then the boys age two and three would turn around in one lane of the double lane road to come back into the yard. This gave them a little more road to travel. They would circle and come back into the driveway. This would make any mother concerned, it sure did this, Mom.

Talking to God, I said, "Lord, I realize I have just received the Holy Ghost, and I don't know if I should ask for this or not, but if it is okay would you keep an look out for my sons while I load the washer and keep them free from harm?" Watching the children to see them get their bikes without any problem, now I go to start the laundry. Just as I get inside the laundry room door all of a sudden, I had my usual thought come through my head, I feel this urge to look out the door to check on them as I usually did. Instantly, I pushed that feeling away and told myself, faith and believe. So I filled the washing machine and came back out with the children. Just as I started out, I saw something I will never forget. A huge man, and his hair was dark with wavy curls about shoulder length he also had a beard. He stood with his arms crossing his chest and booth feet separated. I could not take my eyes off him; I kept looking up at him in amazement, looking at him from top to bottom. I even made circles around him, looking up and looking down at his feet. He was wearing a simple pair of sandals that looked to me like they were made from leather. His clothes were only one-piece leather, looking material, something like short pair of pants with a short skirt covering it and a piece of leather looking fabric from the waist over his shoulder. This angel had no wings and stood somewhere between eight and ten feet tall guessing, could have been taller so I thought he must be a type of warrior because he was wearing an enormous sword. He did not look at me or move; his head or body in any manner.

The angel stayed in my site as long as I looked at him. I did not want to take my eyes off of him, circling him and looking at him up and down. Now feeling content that I had studied him thoroughly; the angel was still in the same position looking at the gate. At that moment, my sons, both of them at the same time, side by side on their hot wheels, streamed to the gate peddling as fast as they possibly could. At this point, I turned to look at them and tried to call them back, but I could not get words out of my mouth. Standing there with my mouth open and trying my best to call them back, but I could not talk: God had stopped my speech. And they turned around before they got close to the gate. They did this over and over and never touched the gate. They lost all interest in the gate. As long as they rode their bikes, they never again touched the gate so it would bounce open.

When I saw them turn around and not go to the gate, being astonished and turning to see the angel, which was no longer visible and my voice returned. Isn't God wonderful? Turning now to check on my daughter, who likes to play under the carport, was interested in her toy and doll she had with her. She was so familiar with the boys going to the gate and me constantly correcting them she was not bothered with what had just happened. But there was no need to worry about that again. They are all in God's hands.

Thanks to my father-in-law, being a real estate broker my husband had bought a nice house. He took me over to see it just before we moved in. I was so happy living there; it was a house owned and used by a church, which had a sound proof room and was used as their instrumental room. My daughter had her own room with all her little dolls and toys this made her happy. The oldest son had his own room in the soundproof room. The youngest had a large room also, so they were all happy to have their own space for their little treasures.

God granted another visit from my sister Beth, which was a blessing each time she came. She lives many miles away and can never visit as often as we would like. We needed our spiritual time together; she was the only person I knew that had the filling of the Holy Ghost other than my baby sister, and she lived in Baltimore with my mother and young brother now, and to us that was like another country. What a wonderful time we had praising and worshiping the Lord and reading our Bible and telling each other the great stories we each had come across in the Bible. When we had our sister time, we also enjoyed talking about our children, and I told Beth I sure miss having a baby in my arms. My three children were all in school now, and it felt so empty at home. She said also she would like to be pregnant again. As we prayed, I ask the Lord to give me one more baby; it didn't matter if it would be a girl or a boy. I just missed having a baby snuggled in my arms. Beth asked to become pregnant, and the Lord gave a message through Beth saying we would become pregnant. Once again in several months, thanking the Lord for this: Beth comes once again to visit. What a surprise! Beth said she had to come and tell me the good news: "I am pregnant!" Then she turned to me and asked if I was.

My reply was "I don't know yet, but I know God heard my request and he said I would be." We had a great time in the Lord as all other times we were together.

My husband came home and saw that Beth was there and decided he wanted her out of his house and now! Just out of the blue, no reason except jealousy. She called her husband and explained to him her visit was shortened and she had to leave now. He said he couldn't come until tomorrow. I could understand that; it wasn't as if she lived in the same state. My husband was furious; he insisted that she should leave his house right now. He took her suitcase and her child's stroller and threw them out the front door. I told him he could not put her out on the street alone and pregnant and with a small child. His reply to that was, "If you love her more, then go with her." My first thoughts were of my children, and then I felt secure with safety and care. I knew he would just take them to his mother's, and she would be happy to tend them until I could come back. Then I packed a small suitcase and told Beth I would come back and the children would be okay.

On the streets we went. Maranda, Beth, and a small child and don't forget her being a pregnant lady. I felt a lot of pressure with this situation but knowing that my three children were being overseen by their grandmother makes it much easier, not to mention God has angels in their charge. Never in my life had I been in a predicament like this. We really had no idea what direction to go or what to do. The only thought we had at first was to let the Lord direct us and lead our path. So we walked and walked and walked, passing an orange tree. Beth says, "Look, here is food." She reached up pulling an orange from the tree and said, "Get you one." Answering her, saying, "I don't think I should because the trunk of the tree is in someone's yard so it belongs to someone."

Beth said, "But the limbs are hanging over the fence over the sidewalk." But I could not make myself eat an orange from that tree. Tell you the truth, I had not felt hunger. We took a rest on a sidewalk bench, lying there was two returnable bottles. Trying to collect enough for the amount we needed for a collect call to Baltimore to call our mother. Beth picked up the bottles and carries them in the store. Then there was a dime in the cement Beth saw it and picked it up. That gave us total of twenty cents for the collect call to Mother; we were so excited we probably looked like two children. When Beth was in the store, I saw a vision, and I now begin telling her of it. As I was alone with the child's stroller, I saw something like I had never seen before. In the sidewalk were a pair of feet to be seen from the ankles down and they were walking straight in front of me as I watched. I could see it clearly, but I could also see through them. We also did see the same prints under our feet as we walked. Mother had a message sent to us that she had it approved for us to spend the second night in the Salvation Army.

The next day, we picked up our bus tickets that Mother had sent us. As we were seated on the bus and the driver took us on the beginning of our journey. Beth was tired and her son was sleepy and they settled in and began to dose. I thought I would read my Bible for a while using the dim overhead light the bus contributed. After a while, I, too, became sleepy, folding my Bible close and reaching up to turn off the light, when the light was off; I thought I would look out the window maybe the fast-moving objects would help me relax so I could sleep. But even though there were fast vague glimpse of building and trees and such; there was something most amazing and it was not passing by like the other views I was seeing. This was a beautiful angel still as a mountain and as clear as day posed by the bus. She never changed her position; she was always the same distance from the bus straight from my window about six feet; I looked again when I woke up, but I could not see her then but I knew she must have charge of us for this trip.

We did make it safe to Mother's, and we had a loving reunion, but Mother was not functional because she had a broken foot. Beth was not there long; her husband said he would pick her up at Mother's, and they headed home. I needed to figure how I was going to go back home to my children, and at this time, I was feeling poorly. My aunt, Mother's sister, came over to visit while I was there and she was also helping my mother all she could and in our conversations, she tells me she was baptized in the Holy Ghost also. I was delighted to hear that. It had been so long since I had seen my northern family.

My aunt asked how I was feeling and I told her just feeling wore out and some stomach pain was about it. She thought maybe a doctor visit would be a good idea. Agreeing with her since my husband was with a company now that had insurance. My aunt suggested a good doctor that she knew well. She made an appointment with her doctor and I being surprised at how soon they worked me in. After he examined me, he asked if I had children. "Oh yes, I do, three."

He said, "Well, this should not come as a shock, the only thing I can find is that you are about three months pregnant." Smiling face was what I had walking out his office. Just as the Lord prophesized. The Lord has given me the baby I had asked for. Now I need to call and let my husband know. He seemed to be exceptionally happy that I called and he said he was sending me an airline ticket, and it would be waiting at the airport. Wow! My first airplane trip! My time with Mother was not what I had expected; her foot was giving her so much pain that she was on pain medication that keep her drowsy or sleeping. It was sad for me to see her that way. My younger sister had the downstairs for her room, and she had a small record player she played her hymns on and prayed.

She would ask me to come down and pray with her; we have kept that memory with us all the days of our life. It was so precious. Her putting God first in her life at such a young age and praying as she did; she was the first that Beth laid hands on and received the Holy Ghost. My aunt and uncle drove me to the airport after tears of sorrow leaving Mother, my younger sister, and my younger brother. Approaching the plane, I was met by the flight attendant and she was very friendly she escorted me to my seat. A few minutes later, she comes to me and says, "Since you are with child the airlines would like to offer the courtesy of a first-class seat since we have few passengers in first class on this flight." Thanking her and following her; I had a small chuckle to myself and said, "Thank you again, Holy Ghost." My husband must have told them I was expecting when he bought the ticket because I was not showing yet. She shows me a seat and asks if I would like by the window. "Yes, please."

Looking in first class, there were only three people in the complete section. Then she returned with snack items. Watching the view was so fascinating to me. Seeing large squares of land that I never dreamed I would see, then the beautiful clouds, and then there were no clouds instead there was a beautiful angel. This angel looked the age of a teenager, having on a simple white dress or gown with a sash around her waist, and it was flapping in the wind, her beautiful blond hair was lovingly moving with the wind. She was posed with her left arm stretched out pointing straight in front of her and her right arm, leaning back to her far right side of her body, her body was slightly turned to the right, toward me, her head looking straight ahead, her left leg was pulled up near her body and her right leg was lifted up a little behind her body; she was only approximately six to eight feet from the window where I was sitting and taking it all in and still in amazement. As long as I focused on her she was there. God gave us guardianship to Baltimore and now from Baltimore. I am sure there was an angel by Beth's car also as they traveled home.

Being met by my husband alone: I couldn't wait to ask him where the children were. He tells me now: he had a girl come live in while I was gone and she brought her things with her so she could take care of the children. I did not particularly care for the live in part but I didn't say anything. Being married for eleven years as of now, I learned through our marriage that was the way to have peace. I tried to leave it up to God, he always knows best. "They are at Mom's. I'll go after them in a while." So he introduced me to the girl quickly as he moves past us both speedily saying, "This is my wife."

The "girl" was a young Indian girl, and she had brought all her belonging with her, even her grand piano. This did not seem to me to be a short-term situation, but again, I was nice and let them take care of their plans. My heart went out to her; she seemed to only have a temporary place to go. She asked my husband about her piano. "Will you take it over there for me?" If I understood this, he was paying her by hauling her piano for her. I had no clue where they were going and not too much about what they were talking about. He kept her at a distance from me and pointed to me and told me to stay over there until he took care of this. His answer to her question was "Sure… it may take a few weeks, but I will get it there." They left to take her to her temporary location. When he arrived from taking her to her location, he had the children with him. They were at his mother's. He had gone all out to plan this; I would surely think. Oh, I was so happy to see my children then; hugs and kisses. Several days later, I asked my husband if the Indian girl had a place for him to take her piano. My husband answered in a sarcastic manner, "She doesn't have any place to take that piano. I am waiting for the right night that it will bring a good price and I am going to sell it at Dad's auction." There was nothing I could say to change his mind. I prayed for this girl that she would have protection and safety and a good place to have a permanent home. That was the end of any conversation concerning that episode. Life went on as nothing had happened.

Six months later, after several false labor trips to the hospital, I gave birth to a beautiful healthy boy, weighing in at eight pounds even. This was not my usual; my other babies were six pounds plus ounces. I named him after the angel Michael in the Bible.

Have you ever made a special request of the Lord? I am sure thinking many of us have. One day I approached the Lord with the request. "Lord, it would be nice to see angels in my house." After asking, the thought went through my mind, this might be something God would not want for me. In my mind and heart, speaking to God, I thought, *It would make me so happy to see angels in my house, Lord, but if it is not your will, it is okay.* "The very next night going for the baby's bottle, as I entered the kitchen doorway, there were three angels, each looked identical to the other one. They had short blond hair with wavy curls, very white transparent bodies. All of them were presented to me except no legs or feet, the three of them were in a circle, their eyes were opened, showing light blue eyes, but they did not look at me and did not move their eyes, just looking forward. Their gowns were glorious and looked tailor-made. The top of the gown had short puffy sleeves; at the waist was a small sash. The skirt, oh my, the skirt; it was flared somewhat and as each angel barley turned from side to side at the same time, the whole time they were in my view. Guessing the skirt to be about ankle length. It swayed softly. Most beautiful of all was the twinkling lights that were through out their whole being even their clothes. Feeling almost paralyzed in this beauty, but about this time, hearing a small cry reminding me why I was in the kitchen, I turned to go to my son and glancing back, they were out of my view. When angels are present it means something. The angels were not there just for my viewing. I was allowed to see them while they were on their mission. Angels all through the Bible were sent on a mission of some kind. I believe those angels were sent concerning my children. What? Suppose I will never know until Jesus tells me when I am in heaven.

There was an elderly lady living in an apartment near me that invited me to her church, and she first off asked a little about me and then she asked if I knew about the Holy Spirit, and then after, I answered yes, she preceded to ask if I knew about being baptized in the Holy Spirit, and when I said yes, she was delighted to hear it. She said the Lord told her he was sending someone near her that had the Holy Ghost, but she looked at me and said I was hoping for someone about my age. I was twenty-four, and she was eighty-four. She was such a nice person. She invited me to go to her church. Her husband was a nonbeliever, and she didn't drive so she rode the church bus, and I said I would like to join her that Sunday. Church had just begun as I was taking the children to their classes and six-month-old Michael to the nursery. I was now enjoying the singing when all of a sudden, I felt I should go to the nursery where my son was. My first thought was, he is fine, and he is in good hands.

After a few minutes, I had the same feeling; feeling again that I should go and check on him *now*. This time, I listened to my feeling. As I approached the nursery door, hearing my son screaming; I could not believe it. Never had I heard him cry so hard, long, or loud! This mother was feeling all kinds of emotions and worries. The nursery attendant at the door holding my son and said, "I was praying you would come. We have tried everything, but we cannot get him to stop crying." She was telling me that he just started crying and she picked him up and offered him the bottle and rocked him; she didn't know what else to do. This was the first time he was left for someone to care for him other than me, and I feel that was why he was so upset. But he was happy after so many hugs and kisses and it took a while. It amazes me the strength between an infant and the mother. But the strength in our prayers is even more powerful. They both are all about love. Our love for one another is usually our first prayer list. How could we live without God in our lives? There were no cell phones in those days, but the Holy Ghost called me to go rescue my son from his discomfort.

Oh, how nice Beth is coming! This was a special time for us. Of course the first thing after her welcoming is praying. It is so amazing the difference between praying on our own and the Holy Ghost to pray for us. When we pray together it seems to intensify in love and power.

> But ye, beloved, building up yourselves on
> your most holy faith, praying in the Holy Ghost,
> Keep yourselves in the love of God, looking for
> the mercy of our Lord Jesus Christ unto eternal
> life. (Jude 1:20–21 KJV)

After praying, we hugged each other, tears filling our eyes from the emotions from God. Beth sitting on the floor beside me where we were praying, lets her arm stretch back a little from my shoulder and she took a hard look at my face. She told me, "There is something on your forehead." My hand started to rub it away, and she said, "No, it is not on it. It is in your head resembling a tattoo, but I cannot see it clear enough."

"What? Are you sure?" I asked her.

She said, "I see something and it has a shape." And then I looked at her forehead.

I told her she also had it and it was the shape of a star. At that time, we did not know what the Star of David looked like, but that was what we were looking at. I was looking at her star, and she was looking at my star. Still to this day, we know what we saw and to our knowledge the Lord was showing that he had his hand on us as in ownership. Telling Beth about the angels in the house, she thought that was awesome! Yes! It was but sometimes when I wake up there is an angel lying above me and I was not expecting that, and around the corners I turned, I bump into them almost and it made me nervous. She was surprised to hear that I was going to ask the Lord to not let me see them. It wasn't long; she, too, knew they were in my house and she said, "I see what you mean." The Lord heard my request, and I was content. Now I pray that they return in my home, now that I am more mature in Christ. Beth wanted to leave before my husband came home so we only had a short visit.

My husband had a falling out with his mother, so he told me after living in our nice home for one year and told me we are moving. "Not again," I said. I pleaded and told him how much I enjoyed living in this house and the children have a good school they attend. My husband says, "Start getting things packed. I'm going to have an auction in our house and yard and we are selling everything." So the auction was performed by him, and he did sale everything even the house. I didn't have the opportunity to let the children or I tell his parents goodbye. Here we are running down the road and not knowing where we are going to live. He decided he wants to go as far away as he can from his parents, and I never knew why. So North Carolina was his choice, and I don't know why. In Charlotte, we rode for days as we sit in the car while he talks to different people trying to figure out what he wanted to do. Then we ride by a place that has a small used camper trailer for sale.

Well, that was going to be our new home. Then he goes to South Carolina and buys ten acres of land with a nice down payment. In the middle of nowhere and that was where our home was parked by the acre of wheat. His new Saint Bernard was chained at the front door so we would know if anyone or anything was near. In the land contract, it stated we had to live on the land for one year before we could initiate a mobile home park (what he had in mind) or anything else plus he could not get a refund on his down payment if he left before the year was up.

It was so lonesome in the wilderness. My husband came and went as he wanted; he had many friends and others. He had a job at a rock quarry, his first at this type of work. But he seemed to like it okay. The children enjoyed the open play area my husband had made them a long rope tree swing and a used mattress under it for them to jump on from the swing. He also bought two shotguns and enforced me into learning how to use them incase snakes came in the yard. He purchased an outside shed and put the washing machine out there. Several times going to the shed with a loaded basket of clothes and having to dodge snakes and each time they ran away from me, thank you Jesus. This just was not my type of living arrangement, if I had a choice.

The three older children were in school and the school bus took them there and back. They were used to walking to school with their friends back and forth to school. My daughter loved her school in Florida and her grades were excellent. Here she was having a problem adjusting because of several bullies on the bus. I would like to take them myself, and I had no phone to communicate to the school authorities. It was miserable for her. It was much cramped and my husband and I slept on the small sofa each night when he was home, and my daughter had a bedroom, which was at the far end of the camper, the three boys were on the bunk beds in the hall that divided the living room and the kitchen from the bathroom. I was not allowed to drive his car (his way of having ownership and authority over me), so he did the grocery shopping; he also made the grocery list. We lived off of a fifty-pound sack of potatoes, eggs, grits, and flour for making biscuits and then the same items would be replenished.

Staying alone with the children most of our marriage while he was out was something I did not mind; at lease it was nice and peaceful when he was out. My mother and Beth were worried about me since they had not seen or heard from me a long time; that was how Mothers letter read, that I received that day and she had sent some stamps and envelope so I could answer her letter. Replying to my mother's letter, I told her, "Yes, please come." Howard after work tells me he won't be home this night either. Mother and Beth arrived this day and my husband was there long enough to throw my sisters crochet out in the yard. I guess that was the best he could do, but it seemed he had to do something to show he was the roaster of the roost. So Mother and Beth spend the night, it was nice to see them; someone that believed in Jesus and both filled with the Holy Ghost and the only visitors I had. Beth brought her little ones with her as usual and my children were delighted to see their cousins. We talked and played with the children; I have missed them so much. Eli had been telling me for several days that he had an angel in his eye. But then he expressed it was in front of his eye blocking some of his vision.

Looking at and in his eye, I saw nothing and I was like my grandma, saying, "It will be all right." He brought this to his grandmother's attention, and she asked him a few questions and he being five years old but mature for his age tells her it is in the center of my vision not in my eye but in front of my eye, and he said the angel is blocking my view. After he described the angel, we know he truly did see an angel, and he did not have anything foreign in his eye. My mother asked if she could pray and asked Jesus to remove the angel so he could see clearly. He answered, "Yes, you may." Mother prayed for the angel to not be seen so Eli could have good vision. The next day, the angel was no longer seen. Early in the morning, of course, the children were wide eyed and eager to go outside and play; their little feet were dancing to get on the rope swing on the huge tree. I was busy making breakfast as the children were scrambling in and out of the camper, playing and running back and forth to the swing. Then my oldest son, Robert, age eight, came running real fast and crying out, "Come see this, you got to see this."

Beth went to see what my son was talking about; after all, we were surrounded by trees and one acre of hay and the nearest house on our two-lane road was several miles down the road. There was no telling what would crawl or walk or slither on the property. When she looked out the door and saw my son; he was very excited and had his arm stretched as far as it would go and pointed up. Saying all excited to "Aunt Beth, look!" Then Beth yelled to Mother and me to come out and hurry to see this.

That was a remarkable day, we will always remember. God gave a heavenly performance for all of us. All the children could see it, but children being children, they were interested in play time but Mother, Beth, and I were not leaving until it was completely over. God showed us spirits in the sky from early morning until dusk dark. It seemed as if we were there not long at all. What was so amazing about the children, not one of them asks for drink or food even though breakfast was still on the stove just as it was cooked: neither tried to distract us as they played. They had to leave the next day and tears fell down my cheek as their car drove away.

My husband while working at the Rock Quarry, there were stories he would tell of how deep they had to dig and how some of the men there were afraid of the depth they were required to go to scoop up the rocks after it was "dynamited." My husband came home early one day, which was surprising; he was trembling all over. I thought maybe someone was hurt at work or worse from the way he looked. He threw down his hat fast and with anger on the sofa and said, "I quit work today." I truly had no respond to that because that was his usual format of employment. He began telling me with Eli listening; there were several that were very deep in the hole, and this was his first time down deep. He said on the stone wall, "There was an image of a human size devil—yes, a devil, and he had horns and a long tail." He told me he had seen pictures of devils before, but he never got the fear radiating to his soul as he did from this image of this devil…

and he and the crew making intimidating remarks to this devil image and my husband said that devil looked at us. "Yes, it turned his head and looked at us." He never wanted anything to do with Jesus and I thought Jesus was giving him another chance to accept him; he did not want any part of it.

Eli does not attend school as of now so he is home with me. There was a small window air-conditioner, and it was dripping water on the sand beneath it and it had made the realistic image of a devil. I did my grandma thing, telling him it was okay, and there was no reason to be afraid; don't worry about it. I still remember her sweet words. Eli was better after I told him that. I picked up a stick and gently swirled the image and showed him it is all gone now. In my heart I knew it was an image of a demon, and a demon was using it to try to scare him. I prayed it would not return. Eli did not know what a devil looked like until he heard his dad describe his story about the quarry, and he felt his dad's fear. Once water again accumulated under the air conditioner again, he was frightened but then discovered it was just water drops and nothing to fear. There were no more issues he knew he was protected by the Holy Ghost.

Not long after the glorious sky show from God, my husband tells me he is going to take his two older sons, aged eight and nine, over to meet their new mother. Alcohol had become a stronger friend of his and his nature was and is violent—not only for me but also a couple times with our children. My oldest son, Robert tried to defend me and it caused my husband to stop instantly. It shocked me to see my nine-year-old trying to protect his Mother; it brought sadness and shame to me to see this. I knew I had to do something. So after the long-term abuse, I had to get help, I started down the dirt lane to the road with the children. My husband yelled to us, you can go if you want but my kids will stay here. I ask them to stay, and I would be back with help. The three oldest went back to the house, but the youngest, Eli, would not go back. He wanted to make sure I would be okay, and that I was not alone. Is that not amazing? He was five years old. God blessed me with my children. About one half mile we walked, and there comes an old farm truck beside us and was driving the speed we were walking and stops after he gets a good look at us. He could tell there was a problem from the red on my face and from our tears. He asked us where we are going. I said to town to the police station, but I am not sure where it is. He said, "You would have a long walk, but I happen to be going that way I would like to help you. It is not safe to be on the highway, you and the boy." He was such a caring person and he was right; it was about twenty miles to the police station. This just reminds me once again that God led my path and directed my life. Once at the police station, the old man ask us to stay in the truck and he would let the policeman know we wanted to talk to him. In just a few minutes, two policemen came out and asked me a few questions and said they would help me and they were all very kind to my son. They wanted to know if my husband was home or not. If I had a place for us to go, did I have gas money? Did I have a key to the car?

When we drove up in front of the camper in the police car, the children ran out, saying, "Dad had left with one of his friends." There was his car sitting in the yard unlocked. The policeman said that some people leave a key in the car, usually under the floor mat. I ask if they would check, that was how afraid I was to touch his car. The policeman said he could not go into his car for that reason, but they would be there watching until I find it. Guess what? He was right; it was under the floor mat. Now, what do I do I thought. Before I could get my thoughts together, the policeman asked me if I had something to sell for gas money to travel to my mother's. All we had was the two shotguns and my sewing machine as I brought them out to put them in the car as the policeman guarded us. The policeman says, you will need changing of clothes. I instructed the children to each get three changing of clothes.

Hopefully, they got what they needed because the policemen were urging me to move quickly to leave before my husband returned because the policeman said your husband may want to follow you and cause trouble. Just as all was placed in the car the children were in and I just hopped in and shut the car door. A car comes up the little dirt driveway, it was his friend bringing him home. One policeman charged toward him before he could come to the children and myself and the other policeman stayed with us. The police talked to him and he and his driver friend left. Then both policemen were with us and helped me with directions on how to get to my mother's location. As we started down our journey, I was shaking, never knowing if he would be around the next corner or not; it was no time he comes to the mobile home I rented after Mother got a job for me where she worked, and she was a big help with the children. He drives up in a car by himself and knocks on the door. Mother peeks out the edge of the window to see who it was and sure enough just who we did not want to see. He was nice to Mother and said he wanted to talk to me. I shook my head no to Mother, as I was still in the house and he wanted me to come outside. He wanted to convince me to reunite with him and he wanted his car. He did not like the idea that I would not communicate with him, so he pulls the distributor cap off the car and takes it with him. We easily replaced it the following day. I did not report it and this was the end as far as I was concerned.

> For all that is in the world, the lust of the flesh, the lust of the eyes, and the pride of life, is not of the Father, but is of the world. (1 John 2:16 KJV)

> So that we may boldly say, The Lord is my helper, and I will not fear what man shall do to me. (Heb. 13:6 KJV)

Years have passed us by, and now I am blessed with grandchildren. My grandson Gene and granddaughter Gina were with me one weekend. They are always a pleasure. I could not help but notice my eleven-year-old Gene kept bringing up conversation about how some boys at school were teasing him and causing all them to get into trouble. He said he tried every way to dodge them, but nothing worked. He wanted the three of us to pray before he went home. I ask Jesus to bind Satan from my grandson and let him walk in Jesus's footprints with a coat of protection. While we were still praying, he placed his hands on my shoulder. After praying he told me he had felt little electrical shocks in his hand when he touched me. God was showing Gene that God is real and to have faith. Next day at school, the boys had lost all interest in him and went their way.

"The eyes of the Lord are upon the righteous, and his ears are open unto their cry. The righteous cry, and the Lord heareth, and delivereth them out of all their troubles" (Ps. 34:15, 17 KJV).

My Grandson's Testimony
The Way I Felt Before and After the Holy Ghost

Before I got the Holy Ghost, I felt like there was nothing wrong with me. I thought I was normal, just like my relatives. But I was wrong, really wrong. I found that my relatives had the Holy Ghost and I did not. Then I was at Grandma Kee's (Frances) house and my grannie (Maranda) and Aunt Beth were praying. Deep down inside, I felt that I really loved Jesus, and wanted to have the Holy Ghost. Then I asked, "Could I get the Holy Ghost since I am only twelve years old?" Aunt Beth said, "Of course you can." So I got down on my knees and prayed so hard and I loved Jesus, that I was filled with the Holy Ghost. The next morning, my heart felt so pure. I wondered if I had been to heaven and back. My advice to anyone that wants to receive the Holy Ghost is to get it, feel the power of Jesus. Ever since I had the Holy Ghost, I have loved Jesus and learned so much, that a regular man cannot teach you (Gene, age 12).

At the young age of twenty-five, shortly after giving birth to my fourth child, which by the way was an answered prayer being blessed with four beautiful; healthy children. My first husband (at that time) and I were RH blood, one negative and one positive. I was never told anything about a blood issue until my second pregnancy. Then it was like a bombshell had fallen beside me. South Carolina law did not require blood test for marriage license in 1964. So I thank God every day for four healthy children. Having been filled with the Holy Ghost and a close relationship with God, I knew my children would be healthy; that is having faith in Jesus our Christ. Before I was twenty-six years old also shortly after having my youngest son, I was told I had cervical cancer, in the first stages. Not knowing much about doctors' lingo at that time, I really did not know much of what they told me. Most of what I did understand was that it was in the first stages and they think they could remove all of it; hopefully, but we will need to remove the womb. Thank you again my Lord for my four healthy children. God can also open the womb of those childless. I know my Lord used those skillful doctors to help heal my body and cervical cancer did not come back.

At the age of forty-eight there was an empty place in my heart. I felt as if I wanted to be closer to Jesus, loving him very much, but feeling that I needed more. I had not been praying in the heavenly language that the Holy Spirit had brought to me and that brought emptiness. So I prayed and also swam through channel after channel on the TV watching preachers teaching; several had some dynamic teaching. Pouring my heart out to the Lord and telling him how much I loved him. Having pain for a while in my left breast, I did not say anything to anyone but my mother and sister, they are my prayer partners. Never having a mammogram I thought this might be a good idea. So once again, I was flipping through channels and there was a preacher from a church called Eagles' Nest. He had a heartfelt sermon; my face was full of tears. He began to pray for people in the audience and I was praying also for them. Afterward, he says now I would like to pray for the television audience and to make a point of contact I am going to raise my hand to the camera and I would like all of you in the TV audience to raise your hand to make contact for your healing. All I could see was a huge hand crossing the television screen. Then I raised my hand, after he prayed for several people; my ears hear, "I see a lady that is being healed of breast cancer." Not knowing who this lady was I prayed for her healing. Then!

I noticed something very vague on the TV screen, something taking form, yes. I could see eyes. Now it is becoming the face as of a man with a head the size of a human head leaning just a little out of the television. I could see it but could also see through it. It turned his head slowly from side to side looking around the room and then it looked up and then it looked again from side to side searching; as soon as he looked my way, it stretched to where I was sitting, leaving a long trail from his head to the TV set. As it came closer, I shrank down in the chair as it got close to my face, its face stayed with my face. After I was as far down in the chair as I could get, I closed my eyes, but nothing happened, so I opened my eyes. I looked up. It came close enough to my face that it could have touched it but it did not. Instead, he brought forth a hand and tapped me on the head and then slowly it returned into the TV, shrinking backward the same as he came. This was a spirit from God, and I was stunned at what I had just experienced. But what was this all about? I had no sure answer at this time.

Going for the mammogram as scheduled and being my first time, I did not know what procedure was. I was told to go into a room where other ladies were to change into a gown then wait in the next room with the same group. We would then be called by name one by one. After the test was performed we were to get dressed and if all was well we would hear the nurse say after the name was called was "Okay, you can go." If there was a problem you would be taken into a private room and the head radiologist would come in to discuss what was found. When my name was called, they took me and my mother (which came with me) in the private room. When the radiologist came in after introduction, he explains to me they found something on my breast and they couldn't figure it out. He asks if I had surgery or maybe a biopsy. My answer was, never, this is my first mammogram ever for me. He then advises me to keep in touch with my doctor if there is any pain or discomfort and keep up with your mammograms.

The only thing I can say is God is my healer. All cancer was healed when God sent his spirit to heal me. God heals and there is a scar left, not that we can see with our eyes but it can be seen by x-ray. I made sure to follow doctors' orders with regular mammograms all these years and no sign of any problem. God is good. All cancer has left my body and never returned.

> But it is good for me to draw near God: I
> have put my trust in the Lord God, that I may
> declare all thy works. (Ps. 73:28 KJV)

Call unto me, and I will answer thee, and
show thee great and mighty things, which though
knowest not. (Jer. 33:3 KJV)

I feel so blessed to have seen the visions that I have. It is His way of letting us know he has not forgotten us or stopped teaching and showing us His love. If we put Jesus first and pray in the spirit He will show us wonders. I love all that God has created—his creatures, earth, the stars, sun, moon, and I am sure much more than we know of.

One night many years ago, I was gazing at the beautiful stars and the splendor of the full moon. I noticed something that was revealed to me. I could see Jesus's face in the moon just as plain as if He were in front of my face. Glorifying and praising His holy name. Feeling so small compared to Him. Now, I glance at the moon His holy face is always there just as it was the first time it was viewed, full moon gives a fuller view.

O Lord God, thou hast begun to shew thy servant thy greatness, and thy mighty hand: for what God is there in heaven or in earth, that can do according to thy works, and according to thy might? (Deut. 3:24 KJV).

During a visit to my mother's, she asked about my problem I have with heel spurs and the discomfort. Explaining to her that it was sometimes in control and times it was very painful. She asked if she could pray for them, and I was more than glad for her to lay hands on me and pray. As I came near her for her to place her hand on my shoulder or head as we usually did, she asks me if I would mind taking my shoes off. "Of course not, Mother," I replied. Slipping off my shoes, Mother had me lift my foot and place it in her hands in her lap. Placing anointing oil on my foot she closed her eyes and was quite for a minute or two. Total silence in the room, and then from her heart she asks Jesus to please touch Marandas feet and correct this problem so no pain will be in her heel. That was a very touching time for me, feeling her love and the love of Jesus and the power of the Holy Spirit. Keeping that time in my memory for ever and knowing my feet were healed even today.

Who his own self bare our sins in his own body on the tree, that we, being dead to sins, should live unto righteousness: by whose strips ye were healed. (1 Pet. 2:24 KJV)

(Jesus talking) Therefore I say unto you, what things soever you desire, when you pray, believe that ye have received them, and ye shall have [them]." (Mark 11:24 KJV)

I have seen things in my life time that most people could not imagine.

One was the miracle of this…

My mother, as loving and thoughtful as any one person could be. Not saying this just because she is my mother but because she was God's child. She was always looking up and praising God, singing to Jesus and feeling the Holy Spirit.

She was the mother I prayed all could have once receiving the baptism in the Holy Ghost in her middle life; she never turned her back on Jesus, always on fire for Him. She always felt closer to God as she looked up into the heavens.

One late afternoon, we were together at her house, she lived alone, but all the family and friends knew Mother's home was their home also. She went over to the front storm door looking into the sky and praying, worshiping God, looking far into heaven. Sitting close by on the sofa I was praying also, just then she shushed me. So I became silent. She began praising in tongues and after some time motions for me and as I began to go to her she waves her hand for me to go back. She said softly and quietly, "Not just yet." Not taking her eyes off of the heavens for a moment as she spoke. Then she asked, "Lord, please let Maranda see the moon move." She told us before that God moved the moon for her, and now, she wanted me to see also. After a while, she motioned for me again and as I got to her, she pulled me into her arms as we stood side by side she ask God again, Lord, let Maranda see the moon move. And as God is my witness, the moon swayed across the sky and then slowly it moved back into its original location.

I am living proof, seeing the moon move for my mother. My mother was not in biblical days, so they could not tell of her experience, but it did happen after the Bible was written and God and I are her witness. Thank you, Heavenly Father, for your visions.

As I was traveling the interstate on my way to work, I was pouring my heart out to God. My second husband had a stroke at the age of forty-five and it caused him to lose normal movement in his right arm and some function in his right leg, and he had lost a large amount of his intelligence not to mention his sight in his right eye. When he was a boy, a horse bucked him off and the horses hoof came down on the back of his head. This left a thin vein in the back of his neck and the blood could not flow as it should.

My son Michael that likes to be called Eli (the Lord changed his name to Eli) was with us when it happened and ran in the house to tell me. Right away, I said let's get him to the hospital. So Eli put him in the car and away we went, I was so thankful to God that Eli was there; he also drove the car for me. We were at the emergency room within forty-five minutes from the time he had the stroke. The doctor was pleased that he arrived so soon. I felt like our second home was the hospital. They ran test after test; they taught him how to swallow again and so many other things. I stayed with him day and night in the hospital for two weeks. His local parents visited one time.

Finally, he was allowed to go home. This was a trying job because he was very cantankerous with me. He acted like a different person. This was on my mind as I was talking to the Lord, I felt such a heavy load, but I was his wife, and I did everything I could for him... Even picking him up by myself when he fell; God had to have helped me because he weighed two hundred pounds and I was not a stout lady. Pouring out my heart and tears running down my cheeks; I heard someone say, Maranda... I was in the car by myself on the interstate, and I heard someone call my name. Then pulling off the road as I was looking in the back view mirror, I thought someone I knew maybe was pulling a joke on me. No one was there; I was so puzzled, and then again, I heard my name—Maranda. I looked all around the outside of the car through the windows, but no one.

Then I heard, "Maranda, I will love you always." My heart melted; I knew this was Jesus. His voice was so soft and loving. And I know there is nothing to worry about for He is always near and in control.

Playing around in my garden—digging, wedding, planting, and enjoying every moment. This was a delightful warm day, no wind or rain, just a calm comfortable day to enjoy outdoors; just then, I heard the ivy growing up the huge Oak tree rattling like the wind was blowing, but there was not any wind today. So I chuckled and thought it must have been some squirrels. I looked at the ivy and did not see any squirrels, and as I looked, the noise stopped and I also saw the leaves suddenly stop moving. Keeping my mind on what I was doing, then again, I heard the leaves shake, I just told myself it is nothing, and then they shook at a lower tone…so I went over to the tree. The leaves stopped moving again as I walked toward it.

Then I saw the FedEx truck in our driveway. Expecting my package, my feet hurried to the house to greet him, he was always a pleasant person. Sure enough he had brought my large bulb the candelabra lily that was ordered about a month ago. Indoor and outdoor plants are a hobby of mine. Having just received the largest bulb I have ever seen in my life, now for focusing on a location for this monster of a bulb that measured nine inches wide. Finally, destination completed I began digging a proper size hole to place it in.

Across the lawn was my neighbor walking over to my yard. She said, "I could not help but notice your bulb and would like to see it." We enjoy our conversations because we both share our love for plants and also share our plants. Then she asks me if she could see my garden in the backyard. "Of course," I said. As we walked along the fence to the garden and walking side by side, she asked questions about what she saw in the garden, and I was talking and pointing to the garden as we walked the front of the garden rows. Now she was a few feet in front ahead of me, and all of a sudden, she froze to a standstill and was holding her arm out to the side. I had been doing the same thing as I was talking and showing the garden, so I did not realize what she was trying to tell me. As I came behind her, she was moving as idle as possible and did not say a word, but had her arm in front of me pressing firm against my arm she was holding me back; as I looked at her, she nodded her head to the garden. As I was looking that way, she stretched her arm toward the area. And there was a snake. We have had a few black snakes before and my son took them to the woods.

This snake had been traveling toward the back of the garden; he turned his head around to us. When I saw him he was in that position. His mouth was wide open and his head was up in the air, and he was as still as a statue. The body was strange looking, having no idea what this type of snake could be. The length was about twelve inches and about another four or five inches long (I will call it a string) for a tail. Saying in a low voice to my neighbor, "Let's back up." That snake gave me the impression that there was no reason to worry, but still not taking chances. Knowing if a snake was about to attack it would show some type of aggressive movement first, at least that is what I had always heard. This one was not moving at all. We did not turn our backs on him; we keep looking at him and walking backward. Heading toward the huge oak tree where the leaves had shuffled, both of us were stunned at the features of this snake and all along I never felt fear or danger.

We looked at him about ten or fifteen minutes and during that time telling my neighbor he must have been sick or hurt because of the black string for a tail, but look at the skin, it is beautiful. She looked at me as if I was weird admiring something that made her afraid. "Look at it," I said. The scales are a glistening bronze-colored background and along the side of the snake were also the blackest black glistening scales that made shapes and even to the mystery of it all they were shaped like an Indian tepee, having four large teepees on each side. This snake never moved not even his eyes or his tongue, which was visible with his mouth open and he was breathing. He did not seem to mind holding up his head for that length of time or having his mouth open and when we had taken the total view until we were completely satisfied; she said she needed to go. So I walked her back to her yard, and we were still remarking about what we had just seen. Curiosity was getting the best of me, only being away for a few minutes, I just had to see one more time what area the snake had moved. Knowing since he looked sick and not moving, he couldn't go far away. Well, there was no sign of him anywhere.

Walking back to the house, thinking of my adult son, Eugene, and his knowledge of these things, I thought calling him would be the answer and at my surprise he was at home today. Explaining all to him, his reply was, he never heard tell of any snake like it, but the tail will sometimes look more like a string if they are sick or have a disease. He suggested that I look on the internet. Good idea, I thought, although all the countries I pulled up around the world I searched and nothing came close to comparing to this creature. Okay, next thinking of the zoo, surely someone there can explain this. Just so happened the person I needed to talk to answered the phone and he explained that answering the phone was rare for him. Reptiles were his specialty plus other. Going into all detail talking as I was reviewing in my mind; he was very nice and tried to be so helpful, he did agree with my son about the tail until… He heard the word *tepee*. He was no longer interested in helping this lady. His exact words were, "There is no such snake." Understanding how he could feel this way, and still knowing I saw this and my neighbor was a witness. This incidence was on my mind for some time. Not mentioning it to my second husband because he had been acting distance these days so I told my mother and sister because we were real close. They said let's pray about it.

We ask the Lord to show us what this meant or what it was. Our prayers were answered. The Lord let me know that the leaves shaking was an angel, which I couldn't see but he was sent to get my attention so I could see the snake, but I didn't respond. Then the angel keeps trying and I still didn't respond. The Lord sent the neighbor lady to point it out to me. The purpose for me seeing the snake was so I could see the shape of teepees that represented my home and the snake's tail represented broken. Never saying one word to my husband, but one week later he tells me he wants a divorce. I knew ahead of time because God warned me. He prepared me for what was coming and it gave me strength to go through it and gave

126

me encouragement to go on with my life. It would have been nice if my husband loved God. He could have had a good life and wouldn't be alone.

By this I know that thou favourest me, Because mine enemy doth not triumph over me. And as for me, thou upholdest me in mine integrity, and settest me before thy face for ever (Ps. 41:11,12 KJV).

Living at this time on a very busy two-lane highway I could not help but notice a very frail elderly woman that would walk on the dirt side road beside the rail road track. Then she would so carefully climb up the piled dirt to cross over the train track. After making it over the rails, she then stood for about fifteen minutes beside the very busy highway. The Holy Ghost had me praying for her safety. Learning as I watched, which I could not help because my sewing room was facing the road and had several large windows. This little lady was waiting for a ride from senior personal service transportation. After a few times seeing her, I noticed she always wore a long coat and a scarf like my mother use to wear to keep her hair from blowing in the wind. Telling myself I should go over to meet her, she looked as if she would be a sweet and gentle person. Time passed fast and never did I find time to meet her. Then it dawned on me, she has not been making her regular trips. Wondering if something may have happened to her... Several months later, her son had moved into her home and he was telling someone his Mother had passed away. As more time had moved along, I was outside and with my camera, and I was busy at work again. I had planted some plants in the leaking bird bath, and of course, I needed a photo. When I had the film developed (yes, and the good old days) there was a vision of the little lady, and she was looking out of my sewing room window as I use to do looking at her. Surprising enough!

There were so many trees in my yard and that meant so many pictures to be taken. I love and enjoy photographing nature. It seems to cause a serenity to come over me as I see the finished product. Looks like the day I was waiting for was at hand; large white clouds were speeding by the trees as the wind was sending them along their way. Going to retrieve my camera; I was excited! Gust of wind was trying to push me along my way as I was coming out of the house, then it started to regain calmness about; seeing the small branches that had fallen around the yard but my focus was the trees. Aiming at each one from different angles and hoping for a profitable outcome for the living room wall.

The almond tree was rather small, the ornamental plum was at full maturity and full of flowers; purple leaves with pinkish flowers that would be a great color scheme. After some snap shots of them I wanted to get some shots of the huge oak trees—approximately fifty-plus years, so the tree surgeon told me. The elderberry tree was still holding green early berries, but thinking it might still be a nice accent for photos. The yard was so peaceful and I stretched out on the grass and took some shots straight up to the tips of the swaying limbs. After viewing and selecting the photos I thought would be used for my purpose; taking them over to Mother's to let her view them since she was the one that taught me to love and enjoy all God's creations. Oh, did she enjoy the pictures. When she picked up the photo of the huge oak tree, she asks if I knew what was in this photo. I ask her, "What do you mean?" She pointed out the large angel in the center of the huge oak tree. Have we so many times said we can't see the forest for the trees? The angel was as large as the center of the tree with beautiful wings. The first angel I seen that had wings as we usually think of when we talk of angels. That was unexpected and so thankful that God showed this to us.

But the natural man received not the things of the spirit of God: for they are foolish unto him: neither can he know them, because they are spiritually discerned. But he that is spiritual judgeth all things, yet he himself is judged of no man (1 Cor. 2:14–15 KJV).

My mother Frances has been diagnosed with cancer of the lungs and also her back. She was given chemo again a few days ago, and now she is really sick. My sister Beth and I took her to the doctor because she was so weak; it took both of us to get her in and out of the vehicle. When the nurse took her vitals, her blood pressure was eighty-two over fifty-four and temp was 101 degrees, and her oxygen was very low. As soon as the doctor gets the vitals report, he tells us that he has called the paramedics to carry her to the next building which was the hospital. She was a very sick lady. Beth had to go back to work, but she did not want to leave Mother. I convinced her that I would call her if need be. She stayed on the phone as much as she could to get the picture of what was happening. The doctor came in and ordered a lot of tests. We were right away praying for her again. She tried so hard to be strong and do what she could to answer questions from the staff. She has been strong in the Lord and full of faith. Her faith carried her through her sickness all the way. While I was waiting for the test results, they had her hooked to every device the emergency room had and I told her to just rest, I would be right here in the room. That did help her to relax and I could see her lips tremble as it always did when she spoke in tongues. There was a small chair in the corner of the room. I knew it was there so the staff would have room to do what was needed for the patient. Crying and praying as quietly as I could, so she could rest. It was hard, though. I thought my mother was ready to meet the Lord that very day. As I wiped my tears away and was looking at her thinking what a wonderful person she was and how thankful I was to God for giving me this person for my mother. Knowing she is ready to go to you at any time you should call her Heavenly Father, but please, for me, let me keep her. Please don't take her this time. I love her so much and I need her at this time in my life. I wiped the tears away again and I looked around the room and then looked up. Not really looking up for anything but just had the urge to look up. There was a ceiling full of angels. I knew then God was at work. Angels filled the space in the ceiling over her bed. They were about five feet above my mother and were standing just far enough from each other that I could see from the bottom of their garment up to their waist of most of them. From the waist up were white clouds. The number of them were enough to go from one end of the bed to the other end and as wide as from the outer edge of the bed to the other side to the wall. They were so many; I could not count them.

For he shall give his angels charge over thee, to keep thee in all ways (Ps. 91:11 KJV).

I thank God for letting the heavens open for my mother, my sister and me. I know my sister was praying as hard as I was. Just a short time after I saw the angels, the nurse comes in to check her statics. Her vitals had changed for the better. In a short time they had a room in intensive care for her and then two days later in a regular room. It took time for her to recover but she is doing well now and we still pray for her battle.

Conclusion: Mother lived another good six months after this episode and she continued with her Christian relationships on the phone. Some were persons she meets in hospitals, emergency rooms and when she was having chemotherapy, even some of the nurses kept in touch as a friend. Mother enjoyed this because she helped a lot to know Christ.

We miss her deeply.

> Let not your heart be troubled: ye believe in God, believe also in me. In my Father's house are many mansions: if it were not so, I would have told you. I go to prepare a place for you. And if I go and prepare a place for you, I will come again and receive you unto myself; that where I am, there you may be also. (John 14:1–3 KJV)

> For the Lord himself shall descend from
> heaven with a shout, with the voice of the arch-
> angel, and with the trump of God: and the dead
> in Christ shall rise first: then we which are alive
> and remain shall be caught up together with
> them in the clouds, to meet the Lord in the air:
> and so shall we ever be with the Lord. (1 Thess.
> 4:16, 17)

All of God's creatures are special. From humans, animals and creatures, plant life, many different ones were created. Being almost middle age now, all of my children were mostly adults and some have families of their own. I decided to shop around for a small pet looking in pet stores and there were many different animals to choose from, but I did not feel any type of connection with any of them. My heart would let me know when the right one came along and the little creature should feel comfortable with me, looking through newspaper and pet books deciding maybe a Maltese would be what I would enjoy; thumbing through the Sunday paper which happened to be available, checking out all the pet ads. It contained a large section of all breads but only finding one ad for Maltese. The ad said, one male Maltese for sale from private home. On the phone, the gentleman sounded as if he was a considerate and caring animal lover. He explained that he did not plan to have puppies but while he was away the child gate was pushed open and they had visitation. This man really loved his little dogs and was adamant for his puppy to receive a good home. He was invited to come with his little possession and I was full of excitement.

As soon as my eyes saw this little guy, it was first love. What was nice about that, he took right up to me. His personality was just what I had looked for. We stayed up all night getting to know each other and let him stay close to me to help him feel relaxed. He was six weeks old and so small; he reminded me of a windup moveable toy like they had when I was a child. We were very happy with each other. He was always by my side after that first night. It came quickly to him to know what I was saying to him, he learned more and more each day. Walking him outside when needed on a lease and then right back inside; there were dogs in the neighborhood.

Most were in fenced yards, even so he was a little frightened of the loud barks so I would not leave him outside. Having a nice long lease, I thought I would see how he would react on the lease outside by himself. So having the lease secured around the huge oak tree for shade and, the front door were only a few steps away having a front door glass to see all his activity without him seeing me. Watching him now circling around and around the bottom of the tree and with each trip around the tree he had less and less leash. Finally he had got himself in a spot that he could not keep going. He became frightened and began barking. Going outside quickly and picking him up and loving him to calm him. Next day, same thing happened, except he doesn't get frightened or bark this time after winding himself tight to the tree same as yesterday he stands still and looks at the front door. Almost chuckling out loud but instead I go out to his rescue but, not picking him up this time. Putting my finger on his neck collar and showing him how to circle back around the tree to unleash his lease. As soon as I leave him and walked inside, he wrapped the lease around the tree again, but this time just as he gets to the stopping point, he reverses and unwinds the lease.

At this moment, I realized this was a smart and easy to train dog and he was full of love and tenderness. Yes, the good Lord gets the credit for this; He sure picked a good pet for me. Well, what should I name this little guy? Going through some names thinking this might be just the one for him, Samson the Great—yes, Samson it will be, nickname, Sammy. He seemed to respond to it very well. Could not ask for a better well-mannered pet; he was a dream. Someone said we have the same personalities—haha! We really do like that person. It was not long Sammy had learned a lot of tricks and he understood English well.

My son, Eugene, was helping our neighbor in her pet grooming business for a while as school was out for summer. He tells me she has two large cats that a lady brought in to have groomed; the lady did not return for her cats. These were well cared for animals, nice cages and fancy collars. The owner of the cats was elderly and our neighbor could not reach her with the contact information she was given and now she dreading to think something must have happened to her. "This lady had her cats in on regular basics and loved them and she would never leave them there,' the groomer said.

The groomer had cared for them several months and was at the point that she needed them to find another place because she needed room for her work area. Of course my son asks me to keep them until the groomer decided what she should do about them. If the lady had not come or called in that length of time then he would find a home for them. Here come two "giant" full grown cats. Yes, and not knowing the first thing about cats, wow, this will be a new adventure, to say the lease. My son said they were both inside cats, oh boy…

Now looking at them I must say they are beautiful cats, the one was a light and dark gray tabby and the other was a silver, supposed to be a rare breed. They were great in the home, not once did they get on countertops, tables, beds, chairs, or furniture. This was nice they were already trained. The tabby was gentle and yet had a fear of a new place; he was standoff. The silver cat had a behavior like a Siamese, very demanding and not friendly, supposes he was having adjustment problems also. They were inside until the silver cat ran out one of the doors as someone was leaving. He wanted no part of reversing that action; he made the backyard his headquarters. Every morning, about six or seven, he would jump up on the six feet outside window ledge of our bedroom window and give a loud yell, over and over. We learned he was telling us it was meal time. So as ordered we would take him a bowl of food, he stood away until we entered the house then he ate his food. Poor tabby was still inside and would stay behind places to feel safe. Waiting to allow him to have adequate time for adjustment, I spoke from a distance. A couple of days later, when one of us was swinging the door again; out darted Tabby and he was gone. No backyard for him! Oh my, thinking of how I tell the groomer her cat is…then it occurred to me, hum, she never has checked up on them. My next thought was, *Okay, seeing the light now. My son has talked me into something again.* He always was convincing. My son felt bad because he was the one going out as

Tabby left. Explaining to him not to worry, God will return him if we are the ones he was to be with.

Two days later, here comes Tabby walking very slowly to the front yard. At first, I called to him carefully, "Tabby, come here. It is okay." He looked so tangled and dirty; I could only imagine what those two days experience has been. He just stood still in place. Knowing he had to be hungry I carried food to him, but as soon as I was approaching him, he backed up. Using slow movement, I put the food down and went back inside so he would feel safe. He sure ate it all, poor baby he had to have been really hungry. After he finished his food, he left again. The next day, I had put food on the front porch for him and he did come and closer, all the way to the front porch and ate it all again. Next day he did the same; this time we had the front door open and no one was near the door, he walked in. His name now is Tiger, he has earned the title. That was a big step for him. Then I knew that he knew where his home was, so he was free to go out and come in as he wanted. A couple days passed, and looking out to the garden, Tiger is coming from the garden; his long fur swishing around as he prances toward the back door, he has something dangling from his mouth and lays it on the back doorstep. Oh my gosh! It was a snake! It was a garden snake that Tiger killed. Why did he put it on the step? What was his purpose for killing it? Most animals kill for food but this was not his purpose. Someone explained to me this was his way of expressing his feeling for you. This was his gift to you. This was amazing to me. The first snake he left on the step, I screamed when I saw it. Okay, and not expecting the second one the next day, I screamed. So thinking he could see gifts are not my thing, there were no more snakes, just rubs and lap sitting. We never did hear from the lady that owned them. So we found a good home for silver and Tiger and Sammy became best friends. Tiger was allowed one sitting comfort spot on the sofa and he was happy.

When Sammy was seven years old, he seemed to be lonesome or not happy. Tiger was getting older and he stayed outside more than inside. Since my husband and I work, we thought Sammy needed company while we were gone, so we found Delilah for Samson; she was only six weeks old, they were very happy together. It surprised me how Sammy would look after her and guard her as a human man would for the woman he loved. If she wasn't with Sammy, he would whine as if he were in pain. They had one liter of four beautiful puppies and shortly after Delilah was acting as if she was not well. They had all their shots and anything they needed or wanted. She had a little runny nose, probably just a cold, but I took her to their veterinarian to make sure.

On the way to the vet, Delilah was in the front seat with me. As I was praying for her that she would be okay, and all of a sudden, the Holy Ghost that was in me was feeling so sorrowful and I was crying and I felt as if my heart had been broken, and I did not know why. Arriving at the Veterinarians office, I told him that she wasn't acting like herself and had a little runny nose. He told me he would like to run some test before he could tell me what it could be. He ask me to leave her and he would call me as soon as he knows. I felt good about leaving her in his care.

About two hours later, I got his call and received the news. He tells me Delilah had kidney stones and with her age and the size of stones, there is nothing that can help her. If we had known earlier maybe there would have been something to help her and as many as she has at the age of two years old she was probably born with them. Our household was a sad place, just as the Holy Ghost was trying to worn me of this moment. Now I understand why I was crying to the vets and all along I just knew she had a little drainage and all would be great. The Holy Ghost has taught me to take heed and beware, but I am steel learning as I go. So now we have to try to sooth Sammy's heartache. Sammy never seemed to get over missing Delilah. He would be happy when we played with him and then he would lie in his special spot by my chair. Wasn't too long after this, Sammy acquired severe arthritis in his hips, he was very badly affected. Our vet said he had one alternative to offer and has never given a dog this size this shot for arthritis, but he would give him the smallest dose possible if I wanted him to. Thinking he is in terrible pain, we have got to do something. He gave him the shot, and it did not seem to help him, he still needed to be carried out to do his business, and he was still feeling so bad, it was tearing me up. Praying over him and asking the Lord to have mercy on him. I talked to Sammy, and I told him I loved him so much and Jesus did too, and it is okay to go to Jesus and when you get there; I will be coming soon.

Two days later, we had to put Sammy to sleep. About this time, Tiger was not doing good health-wise, our vet said he had kidney problems and at his age of twelve years old there wasn't anything they could do for him. Tiger would sit on the sofa and he would let us stroke fur (if we were very gentle) and talk to him, but he would not stay long. He was gone for a few days and hadn't eaten anything that we knew of.

I got an unexpected call from our vet. He begins telling me that Tiger was hit by a car and was taken to his office; he was brought in by a mother and her children. The mother saw the car that hit the animal and she and her children lifted him into her car and carried him to the nearest vet, which happened to be Tigers trusted vet. He preceded to tell me that Tiger had been so badly hurt and he covered all details ending with I would not recommend any procedure. I sure miss our pets.

Several years later in Florida, I thought it would be fun to take pictures of all the places we spent some time. Visiting what was my old home state Florida for ten years, there was not much film left in my camera, but I thought I would take a picture where we were lodging and had so much fun around the pool. Standing nearby was the pool and the laundry facility almost side by side. As I was completing my laundry choir pulling out the camera for a quick flash for memories, and sometime later, when seeing the photo and my friend Peter noticed something. He pointed at the top of the photo in the clouds was my Sammy but not the small creature he was on earth, now he was very large and looked as if he was running very fast too, with his ears pushing back and pressed somewhat to his head from the pressure of the fast wind, making sure he was not too late so I could see him in Heaven. Thank you, Lord. For what we have to study and read in your word there is no place that I know of; that says animals go to heaven or don't go to heaven. But I have a true story that my Sammy is in heaven and God let me see that he is.

"And the armies which were in heaven followed him upon white horses, clothed in fine linen white and clean" (Rev. 19:14 KJV).

We think life is so pleasant in North Carolina. We live half way to the beach and half way to the mountains just depending on which direction we might like to take. When vacation time comes around, makes it hard to decide which one… We made our decision, and it is sand and sea, yippee…

We feel it is best to find a lodging place after arriving at the beach rather than by phone, this being out of season time, walk-ins seems to get a little cheaper rates, well, we feel so from experience at least the last trip we made, this may be different now. Tired from our trip we decide to get some rest and start out tomorrow for fun and adventure. Searching around for a breakfast, maybe a different restaurant from where we had never eaten before; after all this is probably a once-a-year trip. We found a place having a very elaborate front on the building, showy, clean, and welcoming and enticing. Entering in nice double door and taking a few steps, the entire restaurant, had at once become a rundown country scene with a long bar where the cook and waitress (both the same and only one working). Two rows of booths maybe twelve total. The person waiting on us was nice and took our order. After a good length of time she delivers our breakfast and it was a little tasteful. I'm sure she did her best and holding down the place all by lonesome was a hard job. I'm sure it was due to the area circumstances.

Hurricane Matthew had made a mark on this area, most of the debris had been cleaned up, some trees were in piles waiting for pickup and many business signs were missing or destroyed or still half hanging, so many businesses were closed. There was an area that wasn't hit quite as bad and it has a nice shopping area that is built entirely on water. We enjoyed walking around it and visiting the shops, by now we are ready for the car for a sit down. Just as we were seated and getting a cool drink of water, my eyes are so itchy from the wind blowing on us from the water, without any thought I reached in my purse and fumbled around for the small bottle of eye drops and put a drop in my eye. Just then I realized it was not eye drops and now looking at the bottle in my hand, I see it is the deodorizer for bathrooms called One Drop, which is great product but not for my eye. At that time, I will have to admit, I did panic a little (a lot), and my friend Peter said, "I have bottle water in the trunk of the car, I will get it. After two sixteen ounces of water in my eye, which I thank God and Peter that it was there and was thought to be used. Next thing to do was go to the emergency room that was… Where? I must say at this time having GPS was a blessing in itself.

Arriving at the ER and as I was walking from the car to the walkway leading to the entry door, I was asking Jesus to go with me and whatever happens let it be of you Lord. As I was talking to Jesus at that time I looked up into the sky, and there above the entryway was only one white cloud in the sky, it was in the shape of a star and in the center of the star was an opening, showing blue sky that formed a cross. It was right at the entry to the hospital I knew I was doing the right thing; no matter what the outcome would be. That was a bad experience to have my eye flushed, in the hospital; I won't bother you with the gory details, just take my word please. I must say this will be one beach trip memory that will stay with me, mainly because Jesus showed me the large star and the cross in the center. He is with me and the Holy Ghost inside me. The visit turned out in my favor, I was released with a good report of "no damage to my eye." Thank you, my Lord.

"[This is Jesus talking] Peace I leave with you, my peace I give unto you: not as the world giveth, give I unto you. Let not your heart be troubled, neither let it be afraid" (John 14:27 KJV).

Many may not want to read the next few pages and I would understand, but what I am about to share with you is truth and many others also have experience similar type of experience. Demons do exist. Here is one example.

Seeing godly spirits are exciting and very full filling, but this is not about something that rewarding. I was convinced that I had bowel parasites. So the procedure to follow was of course is to see Doctor Albert Hudson and take a sample for the lab. So I did visit my primary doctor and that was what he ordered. I followed through with all instructions and was told I could have the full results in a couple of days. I have always been comfortable talking to my doctor because he is so gentle and easygoing with his speech and with discussing procedures, being a superior doctor as he is making me feel grateful to be his patient. There was about a three-day span before I could see him and his office is about forty five miles one way, but he is worth it.

I thought, finally the outcome will be heard and we can take care of this problem and I can feel free and healthy again. After his nice words of welcome, he gets down to facts. He said he had some great news. You do not have parasites he says with a nice congratulating smile. The only way I could respond to that conclusion was, "Are you sure?"

He reassured me, "There are not any parasites."

Going home feeling a little confused, I just knew the test had to have not tested correctly. After a few days I was still convinced I still had this problem. All I knew was to go back and ask for another testing. This time I was seeing the PA because my doctor was booked up, she is very understanding and we communicate well. She tried to comfort me and convince me that there was no reason for another testing. I confessed it would make me feel better if we tested just one more time. So another test was ordered and I go through all the routine again. After the test was completed, I had returned to see the PA once again. She convinced me I was not having a problem with parasites. I felt so relieved. She was so lenient with me and so compassionate. I just knew all was well. I couldn't thank her enough.

Enjoying my free life for a good few days and the freedom was vastly gone. I say this because now the worms are under my skin on my arms. Peter and Beth and I prayed for this to leave, and truly believe it would have, but when I looked at my skin, I keep seeing it was getting to be a serious problem for me. Faith moves mountains (problems), but I let fear come in without realizing it at the time. Now thinking of the internet as to get help answering questions, as most of us do now a days. Low and behold there were stories of persons suffering from the same issue. So glad to know I am not going crazy. People understand, at least the ones I read about. As the days passed, the worms became bolder, larger, and discomforting. I knew there had to be something that could help people like me. I could not take this anymore; being ashamed to go back to my primary doctor or the PA. Looking for someone to understand I went to the ER at our small nearby hospital. Having to have help, the worms were moving around slowly from one location to another. My feet felt as if they were packed with padding on the bottom, making it so when walking, my feet would rock as the rockers on a rocking chair. While signing into ER, the receptionist asks me why I wanted to be seen; trying to find a decent word or words to tell her, but in a voice of pain I said, "I have worms under my skin." Her wisdom evaluation was "Oh, I know, sometimes they go to the head." At that moment, thinking she understands and they would know all about this at the emergency room. Little did I know? Thinking about it after it was all over, I believe she was helping instill fear into me or having fun at my expense.

Finding a seat and trying not to think of what my problems was. Of course the wait is usually one hour or longer and the ones needing immediate attention are seen first. Completely agreeing with this, but I felt I was one of those to go in the first group because I was feeling severely in need. Looking back on this occurrence, thinking everyone felt the same way. As I sat, getting in a panic and trying to understand they are doing their best to see everyone. The worms began moving up my upper body coming from the stomach area to each side of my body. This is when I felt like screaming, I did not know what to do, I was terrified. They had split into two groups as they moved into each arm and my arms feel like they will explode they were so tight and my veins were swollen. I was afraid. The worse has not come, yet. Some came from the arms and manifested across my heart as I felt it beating rapidly and with pain also. I was praying under my breath as hard as I could, and at that moment, it relaxed, it was calming down.

Thank you, Heavenly Father. But now, they are going to my neck and behind my neck and circling the top of my head staying on top of my head as well. Continuing praying in a few minutes all was calm, and the calmness occurred…now the nurse was calling my name. My rocking feet followed the nurse to the examining room. She was a pleasing person, but she did work quickly with me. As she helped me with my gown, I asked her, "Please don't touch my skin. I would not want you to get this."

She smiled, touched my skin anyway, and told me it was okay, and she briskly left. After a short wait for the doctor coming in, he did not have much to say and all I could tell him was I have worms under my skin. His response was "I don't see any.' I ask him to please look on my back. He took a fast glance and said "I don't see any." And he turned and walked out the room, telling the nurse passing by; I do not have time for this bring someone that needs me. So all I achieved here was humiliation and learning no one cares. I knew God loved me and he was always with me no matter what I may be going through. I might add, the doctor coded my visit as deemed as nonemergency, so I had to write a five-hundred-dollar check for my fifteen-minute ER visit. I went home defeated. A few days later, my doctor's office calls and says the hospital reported my visit and the doctor wanted to follow up. Entering the doctors' office, I found my usual comfy seat waiting for them to call me back. My mind was on how awful I felt and just wanted to return home. I really had a problem that I did not understand.

Hearing my name called, rising from my chair slowly and rocked my way to meet the nurse standing in the door opened for me. In a surprised and loud voice she says, "Are you all right? I never saw you look like this." As she was looking at my face and body. I remarked, "I'm not quite myself today." As Doctor Albert Hudson entered the room, he takes his stool on wheels and brings it close to me as he sits on it. He tries his hardest to tell me in a gentle and understanding way sometimes our minds will tell us things that are not true. He continued in a soft-spoken voice to make sure he could help me out of this troubled situation also help me to understand the situation. Peter, my friend that drove me there, ask him if he had any other patients with this problem. My doctor replied, "Yes, three, in my twenty-five-year career." One is not recovering and the other has been getting better, but it takes a longtime, sometimes years. He was the only one other than Peter and my sister Beth that was with me and handing out a helping hand. They have no idea what that meant to me. Then the doctor leaves the room to gather some paperwork so I could see someone to help me talk this out and bring me back to reality. While Doctor Hudson was out, Peter and I looked at each other and I said to him, if this is in my mind that means this is an attack from Satan. Demons have been working on me! We prayed right then, by expelling the demons. The doctor returns with the paperwork for mental health and paperwork for blood work, which was the regular six month's lab work.

As we sat waiting for my name to be called for lab work, we were still praying and thanking God for my release from demonic powers. As I was waiting, I could feel my body changing back to normal, standing up to go to the lab after my name was called, my feet were becoming normal, walking out of the clinic I was myself again. No worms, no parasites, praise God! On my way out, we decided to go to a restaurant and then Peter wanted to pick up a couple bags of coffee from a well-known coffee shop in our area. I always enjoy going there, they have tea bags, many flavored and they even sell them individually, plus coffee mugs; seeing a fancy mug that read: this will be the best day ever, of course it came home with me.

It took a lot of nerve for me to write about this event in my life and the only reason I did is because I care. I care for those that may have this problem; believe me, I understand. I know what you are going through. Please listen to me because I have been there. Open your mind and know they are not real. They do not control you, and they are your enemy, which are demons. Only God has the power to expel them in the name of Jesus. Faith moves mountains (problems).

For whosoever is born of God overcometh the world: and this is the victory that overcometh the world, even our faith (1 John 5:4 KJV).

Today was a beautiful sunny day filled with many activities and chores as the evening was coming to an end. It was now about eight thirty and on my last chore of folding laundry. While folding and stacking clothes, even though my hands were busy, so was my mind. I was talking and praying to the Lord for a while then I began to sing that old hymn, "In the Garden." This is what was sung as I accepted Jesus as my savior at age nine and even today it is hard to sing it without crying. It just takes that right song that touches our heart, well, this one is mind. Singing right along and then, I hear some men singing. Nothing was turned on, and no one here. All I could do was freeze in position and listen. To my surprise, it was a beautiful nonmusical men's quartet singing a song I had heard many times as a child. "How Great Thou Art," their voices were outstanding. They sang the song, and it seemed to last for so long, no human could sing like that. I have never heard a human voice as strong and hold a note so long. They were in my yard outside my bedroom window. The Lord has shown me in many ways how much he loves me and just as before, I know "how great Thou art"!

> Forasmuch as there is none like unto thee, O Lord; Thou art great, and thy name is great in might. (Jer. 10:6 KJV)

> Bless the Lord, O my soul. O Lord my God, thou are very great; Thou art clothed with honour and majesty: (Ps. 104:1 KJV)

After my shopping was completed at Walmart and leaving the building, I was getting rather thirsty; my eyes noticed the fifty-cent drink machine at the exit door. Just as my change was sliding inside the machine; this noisy buggy was moving by me fast—that was a few feet from my backside. Then a loud, high-pitched male voice, full of anger, and fast speech, screaming, "Stop it, get your hands off my buggy, you have no right. Don't touch it, leave me alone." Then I heard him leave with his buggy. There was another loud, high-pitched angry male voice that answered to him as he left. "It's not supposed to be there, I was helping you by moving it, I was only moving it for you out of your way."

Not knowing at that time why it took my can drink so long to fall down out of the machine, but it did finally, and as I lifted it out, turning to go to my car. This voice I heard was speaking to me; it belonged to a very hyper young man. He says, "Did you hear what he said to me? That man was crazy. I was just trying to help him. All

I wanted to do was help him. I have had it. I want ever help anybody again. That is it for me, never again will I help another person."

My come back to all of this was "Oh, don't say that…everyone is different…everyone is different."

He was quickly thinking and said, "Yes, I know, you are right, everyone is different. I can't say I will never help anyone again."

After hearing that, I said, "And Jesus loves you."

His face became frozen and hard. I turned away, as soon as my back was turned to him. I heard him curse me. My heart jumped for joy. The Bible tells me at that moment God blessed me.

Blessed are ye, when men shall revile you, and persecute you, and shall say all manner of evil against you falsely, for my sake. Rejoice and be exceeding glad: for great is your reward in heaven: for so persecuted they the prophets which were before you (Matt. 5:11–12 KJV).

After a small moment of happiness, I felt so hurt because this young man seemed to have never learned of the joy of living a holy like for Jesus. Never knowing peace, joy, and a happy life, all because he hasn't given his life to his creator, oh, what he has missed out on.

Father, he walked my path for a reason, and I will make that reason so he could have someone who cares to pray for his soul. Right now, Father, I pray for his lost soul. Please touch him, Holy Ghost, woo him and encourage him to claim Jesus as his personal savior. Water baptism and Holy Ghost filled for him to have ever lasting life. Thank you, Father, for hearing my prayer and your word says that if we believe our prayer is answered; it will be done. So I know in my heart that this young man will have a chance to understand you; even if he has turned you down before, Lord, please give him another chance to take you as his savior.

Our friend Peter and I went to a large shopping center in a town from where we live and thought we would just enjoy the day in the mall. We made sure to wear our comfortable shoes; one trip around is almost two miles, but we were not going to be there and not enjoy it all. And believe me, we did. After having a quiet sitting and enjoying our little chitchat, we got a bite to eat. There was so much going on there, it was hard to capture it all. It was time to say goodbye to our adventurous day, so heading to the car and by the way we were blessed to have a parking place in front and close to the entryway door. Now it was time to head home. As we streamed down the interstate, I heard a sound on top outside edge of my side of the car—top edge of the door—it was like a flapping sound of a very heavy rope. Looking over at Peter while he was driving and ask him: what in the world do you think that can be? He said, "I know, I have heard it before." And he whispered, "Demon." All of a sudden something came over me (Holy Ghost), and I took my right hand and roughly taped on the spot inside the car above the window where the sound was coming from and in a louder voice that my regular speech I said, "Go back to hell, you can't touch us." The noise was not heard again.

As I walk thought my daily life with Jesus, I know I am shielded from demonic powers. I know Jesus Christ is my savior, and through the Holy Ghost I have power to make demons run. Praise the Lord.

My life has been amazing, and yours can also. I thank God for choosing me and showing me. I believe one purposes of seeing and experiencing all the spiritual things I have is so I could let others know and understand that God is a spirit and we are surrounded with spirits.

I have also had hardship and trials as all humans do. But no matter what we have to deal with or come against, always remember Jesus Christ is our savior and He is coming soon…

PETER'S CHAPTER

Preface

Hello, my name is Peter; this is my chapter. I think I should put the plan of salvation on this page, don't you? I mean, this is where we all are going to spend the rest of our life; we need to make sure that we have it right. The first thing that we must do is believe and repent in Jesus. Then, the next thing that we must do is get baptized with water. THE ACTS chapter 1, verse 5, For John truly baptized with water; but ye shall be baptized with the HOLY GHOST not many days hence.

Now it is time to get baptized in the HOLY GHOST, only JESUS can baptize in the HOLY GHOST. This is where GOD'S SPIRIT comes inside of us. Let me tell you a story about the HOLY GHOST; this is where I found out about the HOLY GHOST. I and my wife had just broken up so I got lonely quickly. Well, it wasn't no time I met this lady, and we hit it off instantly. She asked me, "Are you a Christian?"

I said, "Yes."

She asked me, "Have you been baptized?"

I said, "Yes, I said the preacher baptized me in the baptismal pool and said 'I baptize you in the name of the FATHER, SON, AND THE HOLY GHOST." She looked at me and said, "That is not all it takes to enter heaven."

I said, "How can that be?"

She said, "Only Jesus can give you the HOLY GHOST. REMEMBER, ONLY JESUS CAN GIVE YOU THE HOLY GHOST. And we all must have the HOLY GHOST or HOLY SPIRIT or we will not see the kingdom of GOD."

And said, Verily I say unto you, Except ye be converted, and become as little children, ye shall not enter into the kingdom of heaven (Matt. 18:3 KJV).

Peter's Testimony

Did you know that Jesus hung on the cross without a drink of water for nine hours after having had spikes driven into his hands and feet? I can't imagine doing that, can you?

I used to believe that all I had to do was believe in God, and I was on my way to heaven until I heard a man say, "Demons believe in God, and they tremble." Then I read it myself in James 2:19.

Well, I knew they were not going to heaven, so I searched in the Bible. I learned that I must be baptized in water, so I did. I said to myself, *Now I am good with God.*

A friend of mine wanted me to live in his house until it was sold. To my great surprise, there was a demon in the house. I know this because of things I experience there. I called a friend of mine in a panic. She said, "With anointing oil put crosses over all the doors and pray." I did everything that she said, and some things on my own but nothing worked. So at my wit's end, I moved out and fast. I moved out and bought a house. To my dismay, the house I bought had demons in it. I called my friend and told her what was happening. She said, "I can get rid of them." She came over and started praying. She spoke in tongues and commanded that they leave and they left.

I was raised Baptist. I'm sixty years old, and I never believed in that. I had thought it was a put on. The demons had left. The house felt clean and quiet. I asked her why I could not get rid of demons. She answered, "You must be baptized in the Holy Ghost to battle demons."

"I was," I told her the preacher had said. "I baptize you in the name of the Father, the Son, and the Holy Ghost."

She said, "A lot of people make that mistake."

"The first baptism is with water, second is in the Holy Ghost." She showed me Luke 3:16. I said, "I want that!" So my friend and her sister laid hands on me as they prayed in the spirit (tongues). I said Jesus's name over and over and faster and faster with earnest desire until the Lord spoke in tongues through me. I had received the Holy Ghost just as the apostles did in Acts 2. I felt so clean inside. Some people say that is just for the early church. Nowhere in the Bible does it say that it is for the early church.

I was born in North Carolina, and I grew up in a small town… The local grocery store was still using sawdust where the butcher would cut everybody's meat. The boy that lived close to me was a very good friend of mind. I guess that's why we hit it off so well, we were close to the same age also. And we liked the same things, fishing mostly. My friend had a lot of land and he had a pond about a half a mile down the road in the woods. They also had a place up in the foot hills, a place that was beautiful and peaceful. I grew up in a Christian home; my mother was the best mother in the world. She would help me with my homework, and after that, we would read the bible, and she would explain everything to me. She wanted her children to go to heaven. We went to church every Sunday morning; we did not go to church on Sunday night unless the church had something special like a Christmas show or a Thanksgiving show or something like that. When people would come to our house, my mother would try to get them saved. She was a real crusader for Jesus. Every time a preacher would come in our area, and he preached the right thing my mother would take us to where he was at and make us listen to him.

> For the HOLY GHOST shall teach you in the
> same hour what ye ought to say. (Luke 12:12
> KJV)

I talk a lot about my mother because she was like the leader of the family; you see, my mother was a real Christian. She was not one of those people that said, "I believe in JESUS and stopped right there." You see, when someone has JESUS, I mean really has JESUS, that is the person that we all look up to. You can know a man and a woman and the man can be a body builder, and he can weigh four hundred pounds and be solid muscle, and his wife, frail, weak, and delicate, weighing seventy-five pounds, but she has the LORD, most people especially real Christian people will have more respect for the seventy-five-pound woman. Everybody loved my mother because she loved JESUS. So the reason that my mother looked after me like she did is she did not want me to stray away from the LORD. And it is easy to do, if everybody would be honest, let's face it; a lot of sins are fun. I even heard a preacher say that one time. But if we want to go to heaven, we must obey the LORD.

> Now the works of the flesh are manifest (perceived by the senses and especially by sense of sight) which are these; Adultery, fornication, uncleanness, lasciviousness, idolatry, witchcraft, hatred, variance, emulations, wrath, strife, seditions, heresies, Envying, murders, drunkenness, revelling, and such like: of which I tell you before, as I have also told you in time past, that they which do such things shall not inherit the kingdom of God. But the fruit of the Spirit is love, joy, peace, long suffering, gentleness, goodness, faith, meekness, temperance: against such is no law (Gal. 5:19–23).

PRAISE THE LORD.

I know I have been talking a lot about my mother and I will tell you why, for one reason, my daddy was a long-haul truck driver and he was seldom at home. Most of the time he would leave home Sunday night, around midnight, and be gone all week, and he would not get home till Friday night or early Saturday morning, that is why I bonded more so with my mother than my daddy. I guess all in all I had a great childhood. I saw other kids come to school wearing dirty clothes, hair not combed; I think that they were just poor. I thank the LORD that he blessed us so much that we did not have to go to school like that. I saw other kids being teased because their clothes did not look good. I felt sorry for the kids that got picked on. I got picked on myself, but it wasn't because of the way I was dressed. It was because there was some bullies in the school. Well, I wanted to give you some more background information about me. I had a great life compared to a lot of people, I think. Every morning when I got up and got dressed, Mom had me some bacon, eggs, grits, toast, hash browns, coffee, milk, apple jelly, and grape jelly. We had this every morning. I just want to tell you how much the Lord blessed us. And it is because we put Jesus first.

> Give to him that asketh thee, and from him that would borrow of thee turn not thou away. (Matt. 5:42 KJV)

> He that hath a bountiful eye shall be blessed; for he giveth of his bread to the poor. (Prov. 22:9 KJV)

I'm just trying to give you some background information of where I was born and raised and what kind of life I had. When I was a little boy, a friend of mind gave me a puppy, we named her sugar. One day, a bad storm comes up and Sugar got her chain wrapped around a tree and lighting struck the tree and killed Sugar, so sad. We all cried for a long time after that. I really loved where I grew up at. Our three houses were lined up in a row, but not like in the city, we lived out in the country. You could put a football field in between our houses. We use to get some kids together in the neighborhood and play football or baseball together and it was a lot of fun. I have always been a happy, carefree guy, and I loved where I grew up. I guess it's that way with all kids, if we grow up in it, it's normal, no matter how we dress or what we eat, if we grow up eating anchovies and wearing a clown suit. We will think that is normal. But I thank the LORD that when the lightning struck the storage building and caught fire and took Sugars life, I thank the LORD that it was not any worse than what it turned out to be, the house could have caught on fire. I feel like the LORD kept the fire from spreading that night; he is always with us. Don't forget to fall in love with JESUS, get baptized in water, and get baptized in the HOLY GHOST.

> Why do the heathen rage, and the people
> imagine a vain thing? (Ps. 2:1 KJV)

> Let us break their bands asunder, and cast
> away their cords from us. (Ps. 2:3 KJV)

I have become a slave for Jesus Christ now and forever. Another thing I remember from childhood is I was about ten years old and my mother wanted me to go down front and give my life to Jesus; well, being eight or ten years old, I was scared to death. When I started walking down that hall, I felt like that everybody in that church was watching me; I was shaking so bad you could hear my teeth rattle. I don't remember what that man said to me, but I said yes to everything, water baptism, the whole works. When it came time to get baptized, well, that's been so long ago. I can't remember if I got baptized in my little church or we went somewhere else. It seems like we went somewhere else because after I got baptized, I remember walking to the back because I was wet and freezing to death, I remember that. When I got to the back where the changing rooms were, I saw for the first time in my life a bunch of naked men. Do you know what that does to a little child that is exposed to that for the first time? I was paralyzed with fear. I know that we were all wearing the same tuxedo, but I was a little boy. I went to a man there and said, "Is there a private room somewhere that I can change my clothes in?" He said, "Come on and I will find you a private room to change your clothes."

> Thy nakedness shall be uncovered, yea, thy
> shame shall be seen: I will take vengeance, and I
> will not meet thee as a man. (Isa. 47:3 KJV)

> Unto Adam also and unto his wife did the
> Lord God make coats of skins, and clothed
> them. (Gen. 3:21 KJV)

I have asked Jesus Christ if he would let me be his servant. This was the greatest honor I have ever had. Ever since I can remember I have had the feeling like there was something in front of me or beside me or behind me like something that I needed to reach out and grab a hold of, but there was not anything to grab a hold of. I know that sounds a little strange, but I could feel that. This went on for a long time, and I finally figured out what it was, it was JESUS calling me. Have you ever been watching TV and you can hear a rich person say, "I feel empty inside?" The reason they feel empty inside is because they don't have a personal relationship with JESUS CHRIST. Nothing will fill that emptiness they have except JESUS. The reason I use rich people is because they have a tendency to rely on their money and not JESUS.

> Behold, I stand at the door, and knock: if any man hear my voice, and open the door, I will come in to him, and will sup with him, and he with me. To him that overcometh will I grant to sit with me on my throne, even as I also over-came, and am set down with my Father in his throne. He that hath an ear, let him hear what the Spirit saith unto the churches. (Rev. 3:20–22 KJV)

I want to tell everybody something. I have heard people say, "I saw an angel the other day." And I said to myself, *I haven't ever seen an angel.* This happened to me more than one time, so one day, I was talking to a man on this subject, and he said have you ever prayed for one? I said no; he said, "Get all the sin out of your life and ask the Lord." Well, I did get all the sin out of my life and I prayed and ask for one: I have seen several angels in the clouds since then.

I have been watching TV before; maybe it was on a talk show I was watching. I could have been watching internet TV. That's a fast-growing thing you know, but there was a man on there and he was wealthy, and he said that he was wealthy, and he also said, his exact words were, "I feel a void in my life." Now he was wealthy, and he was wise. I wasn't trying to recite that old poem: "An apple a day will keep the doctor away." It just worked out that way. But my point is, this man had everything and he was not happy. Now why was this man unhappy? He had everything except JESUS. This was the only thing that he did not have, so it had to be the void in his life. I can see where this would be on someone's mind because if we don't live our life right and obey GOD's law we will be cast in the lake of fire forever.

It says so in the book of Exodus 20:12–17 (KJV); there is also another list of laws that we must live by. It is in book of Galatians 5:13–21 (KJV); actually you might like to read the entire book of Galatians. It is very interesting.

> If there be among you a poor man of one of thy brethren within any of thy gates in thy land which the Lord thy God giveth thee, thou shalt not harden thin heart, nor shut thine hand from thy poor brother: But thou shall open thin hand wide unto him, and shalt surely lend him sufficient for his need, in that which he wanteth. (Deut. 15:7–8 KJV)

I am a servant for Jesus Christ. It is an honor to be a servant for him. I feel like John. I am not worthy to unloose his shoes and wash his feet, but if I had the opportunity to do it, I would. When I was going through school, nobody ever said anything to me about the LORD, except to take his name in vain. Twelve years of school and I never heard anybody say, "Praise the LORD." This country is weak on our relationship with the LORD, and we should make the LORD number one in our lives—more important than our wife, children, anything. I am not a professional author. I'm sure that you can see that, but the LORD told me to write some of my life and put it in a book. I felt like Moses when he told me that. You know the story of Moses, don't you? Moses was a prophet and a Jew that GOD picked him to take all of the slaves out of Egypt and take them to the promise land.

> If my people, which are called by my name,
> shall humble themselves, and pray, and seek my
> face, and turn from their wicked ways; then will
> I hear from heaven, and will forgive their sin,
> and will heal their land. Now mine eyes shall be
> open, and mine ears attend unto the prayer that
> is made in this place. (2 Chron. 7:14–15 KJV)

I am a servant for Jesus Christ forever and ever. It is an honor to be his slave. I have recently discovered some scripture in the Bible that is very important; don't misunderstand me, every word in the Bible is very important, but you know how some things just jump out and grab you. Well, it's the HOLY GHOST. This is GOD'S HOLY SPIRIT, and if we don't have this, we will not see the kingdom of GOD.

But ye are not in the flesh, but in the Spirit, if so be that the Spirit of God dwell in you. Now if any man have not the SPIRIT of CHRIST, he is none of his (Rom. 8:9 KJV).

Let me tell you when I first found out about the HOLY GHOST. Let me tell you about the time a friend of mine wanted me to do him a favor. Let me start at the beginning. My wife and I met at church. We started talking, and then we started dating. We dated for about a year and then we got married. I got a job working at a place that made curtains, bedsheets, quilts, and pillows, and just about anything that could be sewn together and put in a home. I worked there for about a year and then quit. I didn't really like it. I was just waiting to turn twenty-three years old so I could get a job driving a tractor and trailer. Some people call them 18-wheelers. Back then, you had to be twenty-three years old before anybody would hire you. It was just in my blood to drive. I don't know if it got in my blood because my daddy was a truck driver or what, but I learned that I was not going to be happy unless I was driving something, big or little. So I set out to find me a job driving something.

Serve the Lord with fear, and rejoice with trembling (Ps. 2:11 KJV).

There are gold nuggets throughout the Bible. Do you know where in the bible it says, And they said, Believe on the Lord Jesus Christ, and thou shall be saved, and thy house (Acts 16:31 KJV).

These are just a few gold nuggets that we must find in the BIBLE. We all must do a lot of reading and studying to make sure that we have done everything that we needed to do. I'm sorry I got sidetracked, back to the route sales position. I went to a package delivery company on South Boulevard and applied for a job. I got it as soon as I filled out the application that was the LORD that did that for me. Praise his HOLY NAME, JESUS. Yes, it was the LORD that got that job for me.

For with GOD nothing shall be impossible (Luke 1:37 KJV).

It was a good job, it was easy, and the Lord truly blessed me. So I worked that job for four years and then I quit there and went to work at a food place. I worked there for about six months. That was a great job also. I ran a package route up around Lake Norman. I loved those two jobs. Well, I finally turned twenty-three years old, and I enrolled in truck driving training school, my dream has come true; now I'm finally going to drive the big rigs.

But JESUS beheld them, and said unto them, With men this is impossible; but with God all things are possible (Matt. 19:26 KJV).

So I finished truck driving training school. Have you ever heard the saying, I'm living the dream, well, I was living the dream, and it was 1978, this was a great time in my life, the LORD has blessed me so much.

Now that my ninety-day probation period is up, I can drive by myself; if I remember correctly, my first trip was Philadelphia. I was as high as a kite, and I was not on drugs. Have you ever had something to make you high, and you were not on drugs, like maybe skydiving—that is how I felt. Like the HOLY SPIRIT makes you feel. I was driving through Fayetteville, Tennessee, one night and I was driving down a mountain, and all of a sudden, I lost my brakes. I just knew that I was going to die. Loaded heavy, and I got up to about one hundred miles an hour and I kept looking for a curve to show up, but it never did. The road just keeps going straight on and on and on, and I had no brakes at all. Finally after forever, I finally stopped. The LORD was with me that night and if that curvy mountain road would have taken my life that night. I would have gone to hell because I did not have the HOLY GHOST yet. Have you received the Holy Ghost yet? Nobody can see the kingdom of GOD if they don't have the HOLY GHOST. Do you know what the Holy Ghost is? It is the SPIRIT OF GOD. GOD's SPIRIT, this is what humbles us as little children. At the same time came the disciples unto JESUS saying. Who is the greatest in the kingdom of heaven? And JESUS called a little child unto him, set him in the midst of them.

Let me tell you a story about how I was almost killed. I was about twenty years old, and I was working at an airport. There were several different companies that were working there at the same time. I worked in the hanger deck and out on the ramp. Trucks would come in and drop off freight from 7:00 p.m. till 2:00 a.m. Then I would take all the freight and put it on a flat metal skid. Then I would put a net over it and tie it down. When the plane came in from Philadelphia, me and another guy would ride a gigantic fork lift up about thirty feet in the air and slide that big metal skid on to the airplane. The entire floor of the plane was covered with rollers so we could load and unload easily and quickly. Well, when I got back on the ground, I started walking toward the front of the plane. I was under the airplane at this time; those airplanes are making so much noise we have to wear earplugs, if we didn't it will bust our eardrums. Well, all of a sudden, the man that was standing at the front of the plane started waving his arms frantically and screaming at me, "Stop, stop," so I stopped and said what is wrong? And then I saw I was only about one foot from the airplane propeller. It was only the LORD that protected me that day.

For GOD so loved the world, that he gave his only begotten SON, that whosoever believeth in him should not perish, but have everlasting life (John 3:16 KJV).

The LORD saved my life that day. Remember, believe in JESUS, and get water baptized and baptized in the Holy Ghost and become humble as little children.

I am driving a tractor trailer (18-wheeler) at this time in my life; this was what I wanted to do more than anything and they give me a load going to Nashville, Tennessee. I love this job; I get to travel around and see the world and get paid for it. What a job. Well, I get to the terminal in Nashville, drop my trailer, and I find out there are a few friends of mine that just got there also. Well, everybody is hungry because everybody just drove nine hours. Well, finding a steak house is no problem in Nashville. Nashville is kinda like Florida. There are places to eat everywhere. It just don't have the water that Florida has, and they are opened twenty-four hours a day. So the four of us piled in a truck and bobtailed to the nearest steakhouse, which is not far away. We get out of the truck and walk halfway to the steakhouse and find two men and a woman talking. When all of a sudden, one of the men pulled out a gun and started firing it in the air, then he started screaming, "You're with my wife, you're with my wife. Why are you with my wife?" We froze; we did not know what to do. We all looked at each other slowly and said in a low tone, "What do y'all want to do?" Well, about that time, a Nashville police officer drove up to the steakhouse and took the man's gun away from him and placed him under arrest. This is another time the Lord was looking out for me.

"Thou shall not commit adultery. Thou shall not covet thy neighbour's house, thou shall not covet thy neighbour's wife, nor his man servant, nor his maidservant, nor his ox, nor his ass, nor anything that is thy neighbors" (Exod. 20:14, 17 KJV).

You know there are many kinds of danger out in front of an airplane propeller, like I did one time; lose your brakes on an 18-wheeler pulling a payload of eighty thousand pounds, have an automobile accident, and there are many, many other kinds of dangers out in the world. Another kind that I encountered that all most killed me was women. Do you know how I all most died because of women? When I was running that package delivery route that was in 1975; I was working all night long. Most of my working career was all night long. When I was running that package delivery service, there were massage parlors all over the place. Prostitution was everywhere. Sometimes I would leave at 2:00 a.m. to run my package delivery route, and there would be women walking down the street yelling at cars and trucks driving by. They were trying to get someone to stop so they could you know what with them for money. It was really bad in the seventies. This brings on temptation. Did you know it is a sin to dress in a manner that is provocative? When we go out into the world and women are dressed in a manner to where you can see most of their stuff; that is a sin and God will judge those people. A lot of people don't know that.

This I say then, Walk in the Spirit, and ye shall not fulfill the lust of the flesh. For the flesh lusteth against the Spirit and the Spirit against the flesh: and these are contrary one to the other: so that ye cannot do the things that ye would (Gal. 5:16–17 KJV).

Me and my friend, FL, I should have told you this back when I first started writing my part of the book, but I give my friend a nickname, it is FL. It stands for flower because she loves flowers so much. I have lived with her for ten years and can honestly tell you we are strong in God's law, and we live only for Him. I was bored one day so I said, "Let's ride through the mountains."

She said, "That's a great idea." So we packed enough to spend one night, and we took off to ride through the mountains. So finally we came to a town and they had an antique store. So FL loves antiques, flowers, crafts, and everything else women like. So we went inside to look around, and it was a very nice store. So while we were browsing, I came upon a sign that they had posted in the antique shop, and it said camper for sale. So I ask the owners of the antique store where is this camper that is for sale was. They said it is right behind the store. So I walked outside and went to the back of the store and still I didn't see anything. So I went back inside and said to the owners, I don't see any campground behind the store. So the owners took me outside and we had a walk down the road a bit, and finally I saw the campground. I was in the mountains and there was so much foliage you could hardly see the campground.

I would like to say that this happened in 2013, and I am sixty-one years old now so some of these stories might be a little off, like I can't remember if the owner walked with me back to the driveway for the campground or not, I don't want to tell a lie because the Bible says all liars have their part in the lake of fire. I was talking about how the LORD feels about lying.

But the fearful, and unbelieving, and the abominable, and murderers, and whoremongers, and sorcerers, and idolaters, and all liars,

shall have their part in the lake which burneth with fire and brim-
stone: which is the second death (Rev. 21:8 KJV).

So we were just enjoying life so I ask FL if she would like to
go see the camper that was for sale, she said, "Sure, I'd love to." So
we drove through the campground and it was very, very, very nice.
There were two levels; it was kinda like two campgrounds, one on
one mountain and one on the other mountain. There were three
swimming pools, and a pond you could fish out of. All this was on
the lower mountain. It was really, really, fantastic. It made us feel like
that we were on top of the world. Then we decided to go and look at
the other mountain. So we started up this real steep hill, and it was
very, very, steep. I have a circumference degree wheel and the road
that we went up was fifty-fifty on a circumference degree wheel, if
I read this right. When we got to the top of the highest mountain
where the other campground was, it was magnificent. We felt like we
were standing on top of the world. I can't describe the feeling that
I was having. It was breathtaking, plus I had never been in a campground before. So I had two new things that I had never done before
that was giving me a natural rush.

> O give thanks unto the LORD; for he is
> good; for his mercy endureth for ever. (1 Chron.
> 16:34 KJV)

> Give thanks unto the LORD, call upon his
> name, make known his deeds among the people.
> (1 Chron. 16:8 KJV)

I am a servant for Jesus Christ. We all need to get Jesus in our
heart's baptized in water, then get baptized in the HOLY GHOST, then
get humbled as little children. So we found the camper that was for
sale, and it was a very nice camper on the outside. Now we have to go
inside and see what that looks like. Oh, I forgot to tell you something,
the owners of the antique shop gave us the key to the front door so we
could go inside and look around. Actually, the camper had two doors
on it, but they were both on the same side. We had the keys for the

front door, but the keys to the front door did not fit the back door, but we were able to go inside the camper and look around.

Well, to our surprise, it looked brand new, but it smelled bad. FL told me shortly after we had met that she never had a home in her name. So I told her that if she wanted that camper. I would buy it for her and my name would not be on the title. She was speechless; she didn't know what to say. It was her first home that she had in her name that was paid for. It was a thirty-foot camper but to her it was a seven-hundred-foot brick home. So we went back to the antique shop, and we asked the owners of the antique shop if they knew how to get in touch with the people that were selling the camper and they said yes we do. Their number is written on the sign that says camper for sale. It was written in very small numbers. So I called them up and we haggled for a while and finally we agreed on a price. The owner of the camper met us at the campground and we signed the papers and FL had her new home that was bought and paid for.

> Lord our God, how excellent is thy name in
> all the earth! (Ps. 8:9 KJV)

> But the Lord shall endure for ever: he hath
> prepared his throne for judgment. (Ps. 9:7 KJV)

Our story picks up. FL had just got her first home that was totally paid for, and she couldn't be happier. She wanted to go back home and get some things and dress it up because there wasn't anything there except the camper and one of those small refrigerators sitting outside on the deck. I forgot to tell you something; it had the biggest and the nicest deck on it throughout the entire campground. It stretched out over a very deep gully, that's what made it so cool, and it had long poles supporting the deck. And the deck was maybe ten feet by twenty feet. Well, FL was working hard dressing up her new home, you know how girls are, and they never get through decorating.

So one day her sister called and said, "I would like to come over and see your new home." She said "Okay, come on over." So she came over and we got the deck chairs out and we were getting ready to just have a good old sit down, take it easy, chew the fat, and don't forget, enjoy life session. So there we were having the time of our life when all of a sudden FL's sister. I call her PW, and I give everybody in the family a nickname. I don't do this for just anybody, just family members, and good friends. Have you ever had a friend that you could say anything to them and they would not get mad about it? I have had a couple like that, those are hard to find. Now, let me see, where was I. I get sidetracked so easy, o-yeah, now I remember. Let me put the Lord's Bible verse down:

Delight thyself also in the Lord; and he shall give thee the desires of thine heart (Psalm 37:4 KJV).

Okay, where was I? Oh yeah, so there we were having the time of our life when all of a sudden, a black bear appeared in the woods behind the camper. Well, our family get-together turned out to be a "RUN FOR YOUR LIFE" kind of a thing. Have you ever heard or seen tennis shoes squalled like a tire on a car. Well, if you would have been there that day you would have smelled rubber. Everybody was scrambling to get in the camper. So we all just stayed in the camper until the big naughty bear decided to leave. So after a while, the bear decided to leave. He went down in that big deep gully that was beside the camper. This is what the deck was over. We thought it was mama bear because there were two cubs with her. I would have given anything to have been able to pet those cubs. They were absolutely adorable. That was the first time that I have encountered any kind of wild animal in the wild. So the bears left, and we didn't see any more that day. We put our chairs back on the deck and finished our family time together. A few days later, FL was in the kitchen cooking, and I thought it smelled so good, and it did, and I guess who else thought that it smelled so good. Yes, your right, Mr. Black Bear. Yes, he was back for seconds.

In the Lord put I my trust: how say ye to
my soul, Flee as a bird to your mountain? (Ps.
11:1 KJV)

> The wicked walk on every side, when the
> vilest men are exalted. (Ps. 12:8 KJV)

Mr. Black Bear smelled FL's cooking again; only this time, he walked over to the camper and reared up on his back legs stuck his nose up to the window and started sniffing. The first time Mr. Bear came around FL wasn't cooking, that's when FL, and I was waiting for PW, that's FL's sister to come over and help us move in the camper. Now the owner of the campground told us when we bought the camper that we might see a bear. He also told us, if we don't mess with them, they won't mess with us. Well, we were not messing with them but they were messing with us. There seems to be a miss communication between us, the owner, and the bear, don't you think so; I certainly do. So since Mr. Bear failed to read his contract, we decided to make him the guest of honor; we also thought the polite thing to do would be to let dip his plate first while we go and hide in the woods again, this is the second time we did this, so Mr. Bear would have some privacy. We absolutely don't want to be rude to Mr. Bear. I thought about asking Mr. Bear if he would mind helping us out with the dishes, but I remembered that he forgot to read his contract. While this is going on, I was about fifty or sixty feet from the camper FL was still in the camper. That's understandable because she didn't have anywhere to go but the camper, or up a tree and I've seen FL climb a tree, and believe me she is better off in the camper. (A little humor added, we would never feed the bears because we were told it was very dangerous).

> Let a bear robbed of her whelps meet a man,
> rather than a fool in his folly. (Prov. 17:12 KJV)

> As a roaring lion, and a ranging bear; so is a
> wicked ruler over the poor people. (Prov. 28:15
> KJV)

FL is trapped inside the camper because there is a hungry bear outside waiting for his lunch, and his lunch is FL. Well, you see we had this plan worked out to where we were going to live in the mountains in the summer and Florida in the winter time. If we did this then we would be living in a comfortable environment all year long. We would have been in a temperature zone of about sixty-five for a low and eighty-five for our high, give and take a little… While it would have got hot, we would have packed up and went to the mountains, and when it would have got cold, we would have packed up and went to Florida. We were going to spend April, May, June, July, August, September in North Carolina mountains, and then we were going to drive down to Clearwater, Florida, and stay, October, November, December, January, February, March, FL has a good friend that lives down there, and he lets us stay with him as long as we want to. Wow, what a friend. Well, the bear finally goes away and old man winter is coming in. While I am packing up, FL walks up to me and says, I want to thank you for everything that you have done for me, but I can't live in a place that has bears roaming around. I said, "I don't blame you, I didn't know that there was going to be this many bears up here." So she goes on down to Clearwater to be with her friend while I stay in the campground and sell the camper.

"Which maketh Arcturus, Orion, and Pleiades, and the chambers of the south. Which doeth great things past finding out; yea, and wonders without number" (Job 9:9–10 KJV).

So here I am in a campground, twenty miles from the nearest store, all by myself, winter is coming on, and nobody else is in the campground at all, the place is deserted, and I'm expected to stay here and wait for somebody to come around and buy this camper, in the dead of winter. I have done some stupid things in my life, but this one takes the cake. I'm the only person in this campground and there are bears in here too. So I slept in the camper last night, the one that we have up for sale. Well, when I woke up the next morning, I had made up my mind that I wasn't going to spend the winter in a North Carolina Mountain campground. I called up a friend of mine that lived near Monroe North Carolina. I said do you know anybody that would want a roommate for about six months? He said, "I sure do." So he told me where he lived and I went over to his house. I said "I heard that you were looking for a roommate."

He said, "Yes, I am."

So I said, "How much?"

And we agreed on a price, and it was fair. It was better than sleeping with bears.

I am a slave for Jesus Christ. We all need to get water baptized, then get baptized in the HOLY GHOST, then get humbled as little children, or we will not see the kingdom of GOD. I was born and raised in this area, North Carolina and South Carolina area. Plus just about every job I have had has been driving some kind of truck. I have driven everything from a small panel truck to a tractor and trailer, some people call them semi, or an 18-wheeler. I guess you could say I have been a traveling man. Ricky Nelson would have been flattered. (Ricky Nelson was a popular singer-writer, actor, and song-writer in the late 1950s and early 1960s). Traveling Man was one of his hit records. But because of my jobs, I have got to know a lot of people. That is why I got this room so quick, so I thought. I forgot to mention that I knew this guy from years ago. We use to work at the same place. Well, he worked there and I delivered there. He was a nice guy, a little weird, but a nice guy. I guess we are all a little weird in our own way. My temporary new home turned out to be a pigsty. He had a dog that poo all over the house. The bathroom looked like it had not been cleaned in about twenty years and I am not exaggerating either. When I needed a shower, I went up to the health spa. If I would have taken a shower in this bathroom, I would have felt like that I caught the cooties. I actually thought about going back up to the campground and sleeping with the bears. But, if the power went out, I would freeze to death.

> In every thing give thanks: for this is the
> will of God in Christ Jesus concerning you. (1
> Thess. 5:18 KJV)

Well, I feel like that I have jumped from the frying pan and into the fire as far as my living quarters go. Do I want to live in filth and squalor or live in a campground with bears wandering around? Decisions, decisions; well, I have a few friends that live in the Monroe area, so when I get up in the morning, I go visit my old friends. You know you can only do so much of that because they have family, jobs, you know, a life, so I can only do so much of that. I am miserable. I'm living with a guy that I can't stand, he is filthy, and his house has dog poo all over the house—time to move. I call my friend that I called the first time, told him my situation, and he said you aren't going to believe this. I said, "What?"

He said, "He has a house for sale and that I could live in it until it sold."

I said, "That is great." So I moved out of the dog poo house and moved into a nice, clean, two-story house. And the best part is I'm all by myself. So the man that owned the house sends a man over and shows me around and gives me the key.

To everything there is a season, and a time to every purpose under the heaven: A time to be born, and a time to die; and a time to plant, and a time to pluck up that which is planted; A time to kill, and a time to heal; a time to break down, and a time to build up; (Eccles. 3:1–3 KJV).

Well, I have gotten out of the puppy poo house and into a nice, clean, beautiful, two-story home with no rent to pay; too good to be true. So I bring my entire luggage over to the house, unpack my things and begin to settle in. The man that brought the keys over for me said the bedroom upstairs in the center has the newest mattress. I thought it was the most comfortable when I was living there. So I said "Thanks a lot" for all your help and he said you are welcome, and he left. So I go over to the TV and turn it on, and then I go over to the couch and sit down. After a bit, a squeak starts. It does that for a while and then stops. So I don't think a whole lot about it, and I am tired so I go to bed. When I get upstairs, there are three bed rooms, one on the left, one in the middle and one on the right. Also the house is equipped with locks on the inside, so even if somebody had a key to the house they could not get in; remember this, it's important. So when I get up, I take a long hot shower in a nice clean bathtub, in a rent free two-story house. Wow, it don't get any better than this. So I get dressed and go down to the mall. So I spend the whole day down town having the time of my life. Well, after a fun-filled day on the town, it's getting late so I guess that I will call it a day.

My soul is also sore vexed: but thou, O Lord, how long? Return, O Lord, deliver my soul: oh save me for thy mercies' sake (Ps. 6:3–4 KJV).

I go home and take a shower in my nice, clean, bathtub. Then I go downstairs and turn on the TV. I'm sitting there watching TV and that squeak starts again. And I say to myself, "HAY, WAIT, A, MIN-UTE," this squeak is starting at the same time that it did last night. It starts at 7:00 p.m., and it ends at 7:30 p.m. It squeaks for exactly thirty minutes. Well, I am thinking this is really weird. I go all over the house trying to find this squeak, but I just can't locate it. When I go in one room it seems like it moves into another room; it is really weird. I dismiss it for now. I watched a little bit of TV till about nine, brush my teeth and start upstairs for the bedroom. When I get to the top of the stairs, there is a stuffed cat, like a child's toy, lying in the middle of the stairs at the top. Well, I don't know what is going on but I am going to try to find out. I lock all the doors from the inside. If anybody comes in this house tonight, they are going to have to break down the door or break a window. So I put the stuffed cat in a box and go off to bed. The house is for sale so the people that are selling the house have most of the stuff already out. I wake up the next morning, take a shower, and get dressed. It's a two-story house so I have a bathroom upstairs and downstairs and what do you think is the first thing I see?

Preserve me, O God: for in thee do I put my trust. (Ps. 16:1 KJV)

I will love thee, O Lord my strength. (Ps. 18:1 KJV)

From the last page I wrote, I woke up, took a shower, got dressed, opened my door to go downstairs and what was the first thing that I saw, yes, you are right, that stuffed cat. I can't figure this out, all of the doors and windows were locked from the inside. So even if someone came over during the night and they had a key they still couldn't get in. There is something else that I haven't told ya'll yet, you know how I told ya'll that there is three bedrooms upstairs.

One on the left, one in the middle, and one on the right; every time I walk by the bedroom that is on the right, every hair on my body stands straight up. I am starting to get the spooky wookys. Confused and baffled, I leave the house to start my daily routine. There is a small dinner that is only about one mile away that serves good food. The cook use to work at a big-name restaurant so the food is really good. He quite the big-name restaurant and went in business for himself. I guess he did that to make more money, that's the motive most people have when they go in business for them- selves. So I finish my breakfast, and it was good too, and I go to the mall. I have always loved going to the mall. I arrived at my destina- tion and go inside for my exercise walk. I spend all day at the mall, can't you? It's getting dark, so I guess that I will be going home now.

Stand in awe, and sin not; commune with your own heart upon your bed, and be still. Selah. (Ps. 4:4 KJV)

He hath said in his heart, I shall not be moved: for I shall never be in adversity. (Ps. 10:6 KJV)

I get home from the mall and walk in the house and it just doesn't feel right. I know that sounds crazy but it just feels wrong. So I go upstairs to change my clothes and guess what is waiting for me at the top of the stairs, yes, you are right, the stuffed cat. I'm about ready for the mental hospital. I am very serious. I go in my bedroom and take a shower, and then I go downstairs and fix me something to eat. I go in the living room and turn on the TV. I have had the creeps ever since I have got home. It's 7:00 p.m. the squeak has started; it has squeaked for thirty minutes, and it has stopped. It has squeaked for exactly thirty minutes, and I can't find out where it is coming from. Every hair on my body has been sticking up ever since I got home. I go upstairs and brush my teeth and get ready for bed. It takes me a long time to go to sleep because I am really creeped out over this house. At 3:00 a.m. a man's knuckles is banging on the headboard of my bed. I wake up and there is a sheet over my face and I never sleep with a sheet over my face because I feel like I am smothering to death. So as soon as I wake up I go right back to sleep. I wake up about 8:00 a.m., five hours later, and I know that I did not have a dream because the stuffed cat was in the middle of the top of the stairs. I finally realized that there is a demon in the house.

> But the Lord is faithful, who shall stablish
> you, and keep you from evil. (2 Thess. 3:3 KJV)

> Many are the afflictions of the righteous:
> but the lord delivereth him out of them all. (Ps.
> 34:19 KJV)

I just found out this is a demon living in this house. This explains all of the weird activity that has been going on. Well, I don't know what to do, stay here or go back to the nasty house that I was living in. Have you ever been out on a hot highway during the hottest time of the year, and spill gas on the hot concrete or asphalt and after you do that you can see those transparent wavy lines, well that's what some demons looks like. Well, so I have a choice, sleep in a clean house that is possessed by a demon from hell or move back in the filthy house that has dog poopoo all over the place. What a choice. Some of ya'll might think that I am crazy because I can't make up my mind but that house is really filthy. It was full of mice, roaches, spiders, and this is the worse time I have gone through in my entire life. Hay, I just thought of my friends FL and PW that stands for Flower Child and Preacher Woman, they are very, very deep in the Lord. The Lord speaks through them. So I give FL a call and I tell her my situation. She says, "With anointing oil put crosses over all the door ways and on your head." So I did that.

When the unclean spirit is gone out of a man, he walketh through dry places, seeking rest, and findeth none. Then he saith,

I will return into my house from whence I came out; and when he is come, he fineth it empty, swept, and garnished (Matt. 12:43–44 KJV).

So I did everything Flower told me to do and nothing worked. I could not stand it anymore, so I had to go back to the puppy poopoo house. It was either that or I could go back to the deserted campground and sleep with the Black bears. Which one would you pick? So every day I would wake up, get dressed, go to the GYM just to take a shower because where I was staying was too nasty, and then I would just go to the mall. I have had three back operations, so I am very limited as to what I can do. It's hard to have fun when you have had three back operations. So one day I got back home and my roommate was back in his bedroom and I was in the living room and I heard voices. So I walked around looking to see if there was anybody else in the house. I was standing in the living room trying to figure out where the voices were coming from. Have you ever been standing still and two people walk right by you. You know how you can see them; also do you know how you can feel them? That was what happened to me. I could not see them, but I could feel them. Yes, there were demons in that house.

> And the seventy returned again with joy, saying, Lord, even the devils are subject unto us through thy name. (Luke 10:17 KJV)

> And unclean spirits, when they saw him, fell down before him, and cried, saying, Thou art the Son of God. (Mark 3:11 KJV)

I cannot believe what has happened to me. A long-time friend of mine that I have known for twenty-years-plus sent me over to a place to stay the winter, and it was to filthy and nasty to live in. I guess he thinks that I love to wallow in squalor; I thought he was a better friend than that, and he sends me to another place and its possessed by demons. Well, the nasty place was possessed by demons too. I can't believe this; I am basically homeless. So my choices are live in a nasty filthy house that is demon-possessed, or live in a clean house that is demon-possessed or I can go back to the campground and be the only one in the campground, except for the black bears. I am going to pack my clothes and go down to Clearwater, Florida, and stay there until it gets warm and then Flower and I can come back to the camp ground and sell the camper.

> Be strong and of good courage, fear not, nor
> be afraid of them: for the Lord thy God, he it is
> that doth go with thee; he will not fail thee, nor
> forsake thee. (Deut. 31:6 KJV)

> Fear thou not; for I am with thee: be not
> dismayed; for I am thy God: I will strengthen
> thee; yea, I will help thee; yea, I will uphold thee
> with the right hand of my righteousness. (Isa.
> 41:10 KJV)

So here I go leaving North Carolina for Clearwater. I love that highway. I used it a lot when I was a long-haul truck driver. I miss being a long-haul driver that was the best job I ever had. I got to travel all over the Eastern Seaboard and out to Oklahoma and got paid for it; to me, this is the best job in the world, if you don't mind living without a wife. Most men can't live without a wife; I guess that they just get lonely because being married to a long-haul truck driver is not a good life for a married man because we are always gone. I have heard so many stories from other long-haul drivers that they caught their wife's cheating on them. When I was with the trucking company that I worked for, I made a lot of friends that were truck drivers that worked there. One of my best friends was Poor Boy; that was his handle. None of us knew anybody's name because everybody had a CB radio so everybody called everybody else by their handle. So one day, I came in to go to work, or I came in at the end of my work week and somebody there told me that somebody shot Poor Boy. I ask them what happened, they told me that Poor Boy's wife had a boyfriend, and Poor Boy found out about it; so he went home and his wife was not there, then he went over to where her boyfriend lived and kicked the door down and the boyfriend shot him.

Thou shall not kill. Thou shall not commit adultery (Exod. 20:13–14 KJV).

So I am driving down to Clearwater, Florida, on the Coastal Highway all by myself. Now this is truly, truly one of the best times in my life. I am divorced from my nagging wife, I am by myself, and I wish every day of my life could be like this. There is one person that has been in my life that I would love to have had with me. He lives in Myrtle Beach, and the only reason that I did not take him with me was because he smokes, and I just bought a brand-new car. Wow, everybody in the world needs to do this at least once. Travel a while, stop and eat, get a motel, this is all I do all the way down to Clearwater, Florida. This beats living with black bears and demons. Don't get the wrong idea. I am not rich. I sold my house to do this. So when I tell Flower about my exciting time that I had with the bears and the demons. She says, "Well, that doesn't surprise me at all" real nonchalantly like it was nothing. I was thinking, *What is wrong with this woman? She acts like all I did was spell a glass of milk, and I had black bears and demons chasing me. I am starting to think that this woman is touched in the head and that I need to get away from this woman.*

Serve the Lord with fear, and rejoice with trembling. (Ps. 2:11 KJV)

And the Lord commanded us to do all these statues, to fear the Lord our God, for our good always, that he might preserve us alive, as it is at this day. (Deut. 6:24 KJV)

So I go over to where Flower is staying; she is staying with her son, and her son says, "You can't stay here."

"Why?" I ask.

He said, "The landlord will raise the rent."

Let me tell you something about Florida; the weather is wonderful but the people are not so friendly as they are in NC. Well, all the ones that I have ran into were friendly. So I don't have the money to rent a motel room for six months, so I will just sleep in my car. So after a few days, Flower and her son tell me that I can come over in the morning around 9:00 a.m. but I had to be gone by 9:00 p.m. It's not Flower or her son, it is the landlord; you see, most states you can rent a house and it don't matter how many people live in it, but in Florida, the landlords charge by the person, especially most places in Clearwater. If he finds out that I am staying there; he will charge them for me. And also there is a parking problem, you see, Florida is overcrowded in the first place and in most places people have assigned parking spaces like here where Flower is staying. There are only two parking spaces there, one for Flower and one for her son that is the reasons I can't stay there. You see, Florida is all about the dollar. I know that is everywhere, but it is worse in Florida. Everywhere you go, you must pay to park. The mall is the only place I know of that has free parking.

Seek the Lord, and his strength: seek his face evermore. (Ps. 105:4 KJV)

And if any man think that he knoweth anything, he knoweth nothing yet as he ought to know. (1 Cor. 8:2 KJV)

I stayed in Clearwater, Florida, for a while, and one day my side started hurting; it had been doing this for a long time, but it was getting worse. It was getting so bad that I could hardly walk. I knew what it was. It was a hernia; it had been bothering me for years. I had just been putting it off because it didn't hurt that bad to start with. But my insurance was only good in North Carolina. They would cover me anywhere in the United States, but it would need to be an emergency, life threatening. So I packed up my stuff and went back to North Carolina to get my hernia fixed. Well, I had to get somebody to drive me because I was going to have surgery, so I had made a very good friend when I was doing that packing service. So I knew that if there was any way possible he would drive me. We worked together for about ten years, and I saw his wife often. They went to church, keep that in mind. Well, my friend told me that he had to work but his wife would be glad to drive me. She was not working at that time. She had a heart attack, and she was recuperating from that, but she said she was okay to drive. She looked healthy; she didn't look like a woman that had been sick at all. So here we go to the doctor.

> But to us there is but one God, the Father,
> of whom are all things, and we in him; and one
> Lord Jesus Christ, by whom are all things, and we
> by him. (1 Cor. 8:6 KJV)

> Thou therefore endure hardness, as a good
> solider of Jesus Christ. (2 Tim. 2:3 KJV)

So my friend's wife is taking me to the doctor and I told her a few days ago that I would be glad to pay her for driving me there; she said absolutely not. What are friends for. I said, "Well, you are going out of your way and you are burning your gas." She said, "I am not going to take your money."

I said okay, and we dropped it. While we are traveling down the road, she becomes really flirty. Why do women do that? Do they just want to see if they still got it? Do they want to see if they can still turn a man's head? Men look at women; let's be honest. So we get to the hospital, and I check in, and they tell me to go sit down and they will call me when they are ready for me. So I give my friend all my stuff to hold while I'm in surgery. So they get through with me and help me out to the car. I am groggy from the anesthesia; I don't know which way is up. So she drives me home, and I am telling her all the way home how wonderful she is. I am thinking how blessed my friend is to have a wife this wonderful. So we got to my home, and she helped me out of the car, and then she helps me up the sidewalk. Now she helped me in the house, and last but not the least, yes, she helps me in the bedroom, and

I pass out because I am still under the effects of the anesthesia. Now are y'all ready for this, she stole fifty dollars from me.

Thou shall not steal. (Exod. 20:15 KJV)

Ye shall not steal, neither deal falsely, neither lie one to another. (Lev. 19:11 KJV)

You know my friend's wife that drove me to the hospital to get my hernia fixed. I offered her fifty dollars to drive me to the hospital and back home, but she said, "I don't want your money."

Then when I go back for my surgery, she stole fifty dollars from me. I ask ya, who can we trust in this world? Yes, the Lord. You know, when we have known somebody for about ten years and they steal from us, well, for me, it hurts my heart, kinda like, getting your feelings hurt.

So I am at home, tending my wound from hernia operation, bored out of my mind. I do anything and everything to keep from being bored to death. I go out to eat, I go to the gym and watch people work out. I just watch. I've had three back operations, so I go to the mall and walk around; this is a bad time in my life. I finally got strong enough to drive a car some distance, so let's ride down to Myrtle Beach—sounds good to me. I was getting cabin fever anyway. My roommate was planning to leave also. I did not know at the time but my roommate was planning to go to an Island; to visit a friend. When he was in school; he befriended this boy and they became best friends. This mother is divorced; she has two or three children. I can't remember which.

By this we know that we love the children of God, when we love God, and keep his commandments.

For this is the love of God, that we keep his commandments: and his commandments are not grievous. (1 John 5:2–3 KJV)

So while I am driving down to Myrtle Beach. I think about my friend that I worked with when I was doing that package delivery service, Big M. He now lives in Conway, South Carolina. I am leaving the Charlotte, North Carolina, area to go to Myrtle Beach, South Carolina. I am going right through Conway, South Carolina, so I thought that I would stop in and see the old boy. I have known this guy for twenty-two years; he is one of the few people that I have been able to connect with in my life. Is your life like that? I mean, like, we run across hundreds of thousands of people in our live time but there are only a small handful of people that we can really connect with or become really close friends with. How can so many people think so many different ways? Well, I am pulling in the driveway of my friend's house; it's cloudy, and it looks like rain. I walk up to the door, and I see his mother just inside. I say where is my friend, Big M? She looked back in his room; I asked, "Can I see him?"

She says, "Okay." I go back in his room and find that he is sick, so I say, "What's the matter?" He said, "I am dizzy, my head is spinning and it won't stop."

I said, "Do you know what is wrong with you?" He said he had vertigo.

> For God hath not given us the spirit of fear; but of power, and of love and of sound mind. (2 Tim. 1:7 KJV)

> They are all gone aside, they are all together become filthy: there is none that doeth good, no, not one. (Ps. 14:3 KJV)

JESUS CHRIST is my King that I worship. I am his servant, I would do anything that he would want me to do. We all need to feel this way. We also need to get baptized in water, and then we need to get baptized in the HOLY GHOST, and then we need to become humble as little children or we will not see the kingdom of GOD.

Big M has vertigo, so I set with him for a while and try to make him feel better. We talk about the good old days, and the bad old days. We've all had some of each; mine was back operations and let me tell you something: anybody that has had three of those will carry some of that with you for the rest of your life. Big M is starting to look tired so I tell him that I am going to get a motel room, he tells me come tomorrow. I will probably be feeling better. I said okay. So off I go to get me a motel room. I have been coming to Myrtle Beach on and off for years. Ever since I was a little boy; Mother and Daddy came down here a lot. I have got to tell y'all this Myrtle Beach story.

About 1969, this old man owned an old gas station; he had a heart attack and died. So the wife of the man that owned the gas station had an auction. He had a lot of stuff, and one of the things she was going to auction off was a 1962 something or other car. Well, there was a man at the auction that knew the car; it had been sitting in the station parking lot for a long time. He told my dad that if you put on a tire and an alternator it will start right up. So he did that and it cranked right up.

But my God shall supply all your need according to his riches in glory by Christ Jesus. Now unto God and our Father be glory for ever and ever. A-men (Phil. 4:19–20 KJV).

I want to finish my story I was telling you. It was a 1962, something another.

My dad drove the car for about five years and then when I turned sixteen and then he gave the car to me. Well, you know what that is like to turn sixteen and get a car; all you want to do is drive, drive, drive. So I was out driving one day in charlotte North Carolina, and I saw two girls hitching a ride, so I stopped and picked them up. I said, "Where are ya'll going?"

They said, "Myrtle Beach, can you drive us there?"

I said, "Sure," so I drove those girls to Myrtle Beach, 219 miles, just because I didn't have anything to do, and because I was sixteen years old. Do you remember what it was like when you were sixteen years old; now those were the days, my friend.

Take therefore no thought for the morrow:
for the morrow shall take thought for the things

of itself. Sufficient unto the day is the evil thereof.
(Matt. 6:34 KJV)

Wherefor by their fruits ye shall know them.
(Matt. 7:20 KJV)

Ever since I got the Holy Ghost. I have had so many things open
up to me. Have you ever heard that song "Amazing Grace": "T'was
blind but now I see?" When you or anybody receives the Holy Ghost,
you will see things that you have never seen before. I know how that
sounds but I am telling you the truth. You women can understand
this more so than you men, it is like having a baby; the Holy Ghost
is put inside you from Jesus Christ. Then it starts to grow just like
a baby, but if you or we, I mean everybody in the world, goes back
into sin, your light will grow dim. Your light is the Holy Ghost. You
women have to feed your baby, don't you? Well, you must feed the
Holy Ghost by reading your Bible and worshipping. We must show
the Lord our God that we want him more than anything. And don't
you believe once saved always saved. Do you think for one minute
you can ask God to save you and then you can go back into sin and
go to heaven? You know the Lord our God sent Moses up to the top
of Mt. Sinai to write the Ten Commandments, and they were chis-
eled in stone; Moses had to carry those two stone tablets down Mt.
Sinai and what were the people doing when he got to the bottom of
the mountain, dancing naked around a golden calf.

Thou shall not commit adultery. Thou shall not steal (Exod.
20:14, 15 KJV).

My daddy had a friend that worked with him at the first trucking company that he worked for; my daddy called him Ryder. I think
that was his CB handle. In the trucking industry, most people called
all their friends by their CB handle. They were very good friends.
The reason that I know this is because my daddy would go over to
his house and my daddy would have him over to our house. Daddy
would not do that unless he liked the person a lot or they were family.
One day, Ryder, had a heart attack. Well, the paramedics were called
out to the place where Ryder had his heart attack and they rushed

him to the hospital. While Ryder was on the operating table, his spirit came out of his body. He told me that his spirit floated up to the ceiling and it hovered like a helicopter. He said that he could look down and watch the doctors operating on him. Well, when they got through Ryder's spirit went back in his body and he got okay and he finished out his life.

> And as it is appointed unto men once to die, but after this the judgement. (Heb. 9:27 KJV)

> Then shall the dust return to the earth as it was: and the spirit shall return unto God who gave it. (Eccles. 12:7 KJV)

> His breath goeth forth, he returneth to his earth; in that very day his thoughts perish. (Ps. 146:4 KJV)

One day, as I was out working, this was when I was delivering packages, I came across a man and he struck up conservation with me. He acted like he wanted to talk, and ya'll know how unusual that is. Most people are in a hurry and don't want to talk to anybody. I guess most people want to get home quick because most people have a wife and kids. I guess this guy didn't have a wife or kids, or maybe he and his wife weren't getting along.

Anyway, I could tell that this guy had something on his mind and he wanted to tell somebody. Well, we small talked for a while, and then he finally got to what he wanted to talk about. He told me he was driving down the road the other day, and he was starting to die. He said that he pulled over on the side of the road, turned his car off, and then, he got out of his car and started walking down into the woods. He said that he parked his car at an area there was a lot of woods. He said that he fell to his knees and started praying. After praying for a while, the Lord came to him. The man that was dying told the Lord, "If you will give me one more chance, I will do better." So the man didn't die, so I guess that the Lord knew that the man would do better. If anybody has the Holy Ghost, the Lord will give you physical confirmation.

> Seek the Lord and his strength, seek his face continually. (1 Chron. 16:11 KJV)

> So when they had dined, Jesus saith to Simon Peter, Simon, son of Jonas, lovest thou me more than these? He saith unto him, Yea, Lord; thou knowest that I love thee. He saith unto him, Feed my lambs. He saith to him again the second time, Simon, son of Jonas, lovest thou me? He saith unto him, Yea, Lord; thou knowest that I love thee. He saith unto him, Feed my sheep. He saith unto him the third time, Simon, son of Jonas, lovest thou me? Peter was grived because he said unto him the third time, Lovest thou me? And he said unto him, Lord, thou knowest all things; thou knowest that I love thee. Jesus said unto him, Feed my sheep. (John 21:15–17 KJV)

When we get the Holy Ghost, the Lord will show us things that we can't imagine. I was driving down the road a few days ago, and I looked up in the sky, and you won't believe what I saw. I saw a Doberman Pincher sitting on a cloud, and he turned his head to look at me. No, I don't use drugs, nor do I consume alcohol. When we get God's Spirit, this is the Holy Ghost inside of us; he shows us things in a spirit world, I know this for a fact. I lived in three houses that were occupied by demons; I saw them. One of them, I could only see his legs, they were blue. Another one, I could only hear him, he was the one banging his knuckles on the headboard of my bead. The other two were standing right beside of me talking. I could not see them, they were in spirit, but I could feel their presents.

For by him were all things created, that are in heaven, and that are in earth, visible and invisible, whether they be thrones, or dominions, or principalities, or powers: all things were created by him, and for him: And he is before all things, and by him all things consist (Col. 1:16, 17 KJV).

Also we need to feed his sheep, feed people his Word of God. I have told ya'll some stories regarding the SPIRIT world; well, I have another story to tell ya'll. Me and a friend of mine—well, its Flower—we have known each other for a long time, and actually, she is the one that helped me get the Holy Ghost. Well, you know how it is when you have known someone for a long time, you can say almost anything to them and they don't care.

So one day we were talking and I called her a wabbit, that's "rabbit." So it got to be a habit. Do you get it, "habbit, rabbit, wabbit," little joke. So after a while, Flower started calling me wabbit. So one day, Flower and I were driving down the road and I looked up in the sky and we saw two bunny wabbits sitting in the sky side by side reading a Bible. Yes, the two bunny wabbits were sitting side by side, holding a Bible as if they were reading it. We were so amazed when we saw that. Everything I have written down in this book is the truth. And don't let anybody tell you different. A lot of people would not believe the things I have written in my chapter, but I can prove it to you. If you are sinning in anyway, if you are smoking, drinking, using drugs, stop it all. Get the Holy Ghost and the Lord will show you things you won't believe.

Give unto the Lord, O ye mighty, give unto
the Lord glory and strength. (Ps. 29:1 KJV)

Praise the Lord.

My mother was a good God-fearing woman. She took us to Sunday school and church every Sunday. If a preacher was having a crusade, we went to it, or we watched it on TV. She did her best to see that her children were saved and going to heaven. That was not meant as an arrogant statement. We must be humbled as little children and holy, without sin, to go to heaven. And even then, we are at the Lord's mercy. Praise the Lord. She read her Bible to us every day. All her life, she lived for the Lord, about fifty years. When my wife and I broke up, I met this lady; she is the one I call Flower. I wrote a lot about Flower earlier in my chapter. We didn't know about the Holy Ghost because the churches that we went to didn't preach about the Holy Ghost. Flower told me that we have to have the Holy Ghost, or we will not see the kingdom of God. I was worried about my mother because she had died before she got the chance to receive the Holy Ghost. And I have heard preachers and teachers and TV evangelists say that when somebody goes to hell, there is no coming out of that place. So I started praying to our Lord. I prayed night after night for some time. I don't exactly know how long I prayed, but one day we were having prayer meeting and the Lord spoke and said, "I have gone to hell and pulled your mother out." What a wonderful Lord we have. These are the things that we can experience when we have the baptism of the Holy Ghost and stop sinning.

About the Authors

Maranda, a young wife and mother, thinking she had been sealed for heaven, but then receiving the Holy Spirit in her life, entered another world, a world she never knew exist. The very day after being filled with the Holy Spirit, in her yard two feet from her was a giant of an angel that was guarding her sons from danger. God has allowed the viewing of many angels and visions along with other family members that are also spirit-filled. She would like to share the wonders of God with all. Have you asked God to let you see angels? She did.

Beth was a teenager runaway and wondered if there was a god. While living amongst hippies, she went in search to see if a god really exists. After some time, she gave up her search and joined a motorcycle club. God took her on a journey that will open up her heart and mind in a way she could never have guessed. Her first thought was to share with her mother and sibling about this wonderful experience but was afraid they would not believe her.

CPSIA information can be obtained
at www.ICGtesting.com
Printed in the USA
JSHW021154050323
38440JS00001B/7